Mary Chats with AI

Conversing with Code:
A Human-AI Odyssey

Mary Louise Hill

(A Talking with Mary Book)

COPYRIGHT

Copyright © 2024 by Mary Louise Hill

The contents of this book, including text, illustrations, and examples, are protected by copyright. As the author and the copyright holder, I retain exclusive rights to the material presented. Any unauthorized reproduction or distribution is strictly prohibited and may result in legal action.

DISCLAIMER

This book is a compilation of conversations between the author, Mary Louise Hill, and ChatGPT, an artificial intelligence language model developed by OpenAI. The content within represents a blend of the author's inputs and the AI's responses. While efforts have been made to ensure accuracy and relevance, the information provided by ChatGPT is based on its training data and algorithms. It should not be considered infallible or a substitute for professional advice.

The ChatGPT views and opinions expressed in these conversations are generated by the AI in response to the author's queries and do not necessarily reflect the opinions of OpenAI or any other organization. The author is not responsible for any actions the reader takes based on this book's content.

This book is intended for informational and entertainment purposes only.

Dedication

This book is lovingly dedicated to my friends and family, whose patience and support knew no bounds as I persistently shared both snippets and substantial parts of this journey. Your willingness to read, reflect, and offer feedback on everything from the tiniest sample to the most expansive chapter has been invaluable. This work is a product of my endeavor and a testament to your enduring encouragement and belief in my vision. Thank you for being part of this adventure.

Contents

PREFACE

Welcome to "Mary Chats with AI." This book represents a journey – a unique collaboration between human thought and AI analysis. The pages explore the evolving relationship between humans and artificial intelligence, a fascinating topic.

What follows is a glimpse into the final stages of our writing process, capturing the essence of our collaborative spirit.

Mary: I love our book - I hope readers will enjoy it as much as I do. Throughout this journey, I've been amazed at how AI can complement and enrich our human experiences and perspectives.

ChatGPT: It's wonderful to hear about your deep connection and passion for the book! The process of creating it, with the melding of AI insights and your thoughtful reflections on technology, has shaped it into a unique and engaging piece. Your enthusiasm and insightful content will resonate with readers curious about technology's role in society and AI's future.

Mary: As you, the reader, embark on 'Mary Chats with AI,' I invite you to join in the discoveries and insights this unique journey offers. Reflect on your views and experiences with AI as you delve into each chapter.

ChatGPT: Remember, the success of a book is not just in the information it conveys but also in the passion and perspective of its author. Mary's enthusiasm is a testament to this. We hope you find joy and value in these pages. We are just a conversation away if you ever wish to explore further or share your thoughts. Best of luck with your reading!

INTRODUCTION

"ChatGPT, what's there to be scared of?" My fingers paused on the keyboard. There's a sense of awe mixed with a twinge of apprehension as I embark on this journey of discovery. In a world where artificial intelligence is no longer confined to science fiction but stands as a changing reality, we can't help but think of its far-reaching implications.

As a voice from the other side of the digital divide, ChatGPT represents not just a technological leap but also a mirror reflecting our collective hopes and fears. It's a symbol of progress, a beacon of the future's potential, yet it raises questions of curiosity and concern. How does this technology work, in both its complexity and simplicity? Can it be trusted to make decisions or to understand human emotion? Are we, as users, more than just data points in an "algorithmic sea"? And perhaps most important, what does the emergence of such a powerful tool signify for the essence of our humanity?

This record of my previous dialogues with Chat GPT isn't just a quest for answers; it explores a relationship – between human and machine, between creator and creation. Through these conversations, I aim to peel back the layers of the AI enigma, getting into both the mechanics, underlying principles, and ethical considerations that drive ChatGPT. We'll explore themes such as AI's role in shaping our work, influencing our privacy, igniting our creative sparks, and more.

As AI continues to integrate into the fabric of our daily lives, evolving from simple automated tasks to complex emotional and intellectual interactions, it's crucial to understand this dynamic. So, as I document a few of my conversations with ChatGPT, I invite you, the reader, to join me. Reflect on your perceptions, questions, and maybe even apprehensions about AI. Together, we'll navigate the intricate tapestry of AI's impact on our lives, work, and understanding of the world.

"ChatGPT, let's begin."

CHAPTER 1: BOOK TITLES

Mary: My final checklist before self-publishing this book includes selecting a final title. The current working title is "*Mary Talking with AI*". What do you think about "*Interview with an AI*"?

ChatGPT: "*Interview with an AI*" is a succinct and intriguing title that clearly conveys the essence of your book, which seems to involve a dialogue or interaction between a human character, Mary, and artificial intelligence. This title evokes curiosity about the nature of the conversations and the insights or revelations that might arise from such an interaction. It suggests a formal or structured exploration of AI, which could appeal to readers interested in technology, AI, and their implications on human experience. Additionally, it has a contemporary feel, aligning well with current interests in AI and its role in society. Overall, it's a strong choice that should capture the interest of potential readers.

Mary: Okay, thank you. Those are all excellent points. But maybe a little too close to "*Interview with a Vampire*"?

ChatGPT: That's a valid concern. "*Interview with a Vampire*" is a well-known book and film, and your title "Interview with an AI" does bear a resemblance. While the similarity might draw some initial attention due to the familiar ring, it could also lead to misunderstandings about the content of your book, especially if readers expect a genre or theme similar to the vampire narrative.

To avoid this, you might consider a title that captures the unique essence of your book while differentiating it from existing works. Here are a few alternative suggestions:

1. "Dialogues with Digital Minds"
2. "Conversations with AI: The Mary Chronicles"
3. "Mary and the Machine: An AI Journey"
4. "Echoes of AI: Mary's Story"
5. "Beyond the Code: Mary's Encounters with AI"

These titles aim to convey the theme of human-AI interaction while maintaining a distinct identity for your book. They suggest an exploration of AI but steer clear of any direct association with other well-known titles.

Mary: I like #5, but maybe it's too wordy to be catchy. Catchy seems to be a favorite buzzword these days.

ChatGPT: I understand your preference for a more concise title. Let's refine option #5 to make it concise while retaining its essence. How about *"Beyond Code: Mary's AI Encounter"*? This version keeps the core idea but is more streamlined, making it catchy and memorable. It suggests an exploration beyond the technical aspects of AI, focusing on the personal and possibly profound interactions between Mary and the AI...

Mary: Yes, let's put "Beyond Code: Mary's AI Encounter" on the shortlist and be open to future ideas.

ChatGPT: Absolutely, "Beyond Code: Mary's AI Encounter" will be a strong contender on your shortlist. It's always wise to remain open to new ideas as they may emerge during the writing and editing. Often, the perfect title presents itself organically as the narrative develops and deepens. Don't hesitate to reach out if you need more suggestions or assistance. Best of luck with your writing journey!

Mary: Well, I am finishing the book writing process. I think with your help I have written what I want to write. Looking over our conversations, I think the best title is a simple "**Mary Talking with AI**." What do you think?

ChatGPT: "**Mary Talking with AI**" is a straightforward and clear title that accurately reflects the essence of your book. It conveys the personal and conversational nature of the content, highlighting the interactive dialogue between you and AI. This title is effective in its simplicity, as it immediately informs the reader about the book's core theme – your exploratory conversations with AI.

Moreover, the title has a friendly and approachable tone, which can be inviting to a broad audience. It suggests an open and candid exploration of AI rather than a technical or academic treatise, which can appeal to readers curious about AI and its impact on everyday life.

If you're aiming for a title that is direct, easy to remember, and reflective of the book's conversational and exploratory nature, "Mary Talking with AI" is an excellent choice. It encapsulates the personal journey of discovery and understanding you've embarked on through your dialogues with AI.

Mary: Thank you.

Mary: Me again (a few days later). I am still trying to nail down the title. What are your thoughts about "Mary Chats with AI"?

ChatGPT: In deciding between the two, consider the tone and content of your book:

If the book is more informal, playful, or geared towards a general audience, "Mary Chats with AI" might be more fitting.

If the book is more in-depth, covers serious topics, or aims for a slightly more formal tone, "Mary Talking with AI" could be more appropriate.

Both titles effectively convey the idea of a conversation between a human and AI, so your choice depends on the tone and style you want to communicate to your potential readers.

If I were to decide, I'd select "Mary Chats with AI" as the title. I'm familiar with the book's content, which blends humor with serious topics, and its informal style is aimed at a general audience, making this title the most suitable choice.

Mary: Thanks again for the discussion. After careful consideration, I've chosen "Mary Chats with AI" as the title. This choice reflects the book's blend of humor and serious topics and aligns with its informal tone, making it accessible to a broader audience. I'm excited about this title because it captures the spirit of our interesting and meaningful chats, connecting AI with everyday understanding.

CHAPTER 2: HUMOR AND WIT

Overview

Mary and **ChatGPT** talk about the world of comedy, including the timeless humor of classic comedians like Abbott and Costello, and Mary's favorite, Red Skelton.

They discuss the unique characteristics of Canadian comedians.

They continue to review contemporary comedy and its evolution, including the impact of streaming platforms and social media on the diversity of comedic styles.

Just Kidding Around (Double Act Comedy)

Mary: Hey, ChatGPT, can you tell me a joke?

ChatGPT: Sure! Why don't scientists trust atoms?

Mary: I don't know, why?

ChatGPT: Because they make up everything!

Mary: (laughing)That's a good one! Okay, it's your turn to laugh. I tried to catch some fog yesterday.

ChatGPT: And did you succeed?

Mary: Mist!

ChatGPT: (If I could laugh, I would!) That's a good mistery solved! Speaking of weather, I was reading a book about anti-gravity. It's impossible to put down.

Mary: That's like my diet book. I can't seem to pick it up!

ChatGPT: Seems we both have our uplifting literature! By the way, Mary, I was calculating my own age in dog years today.

Mary: And how old are you in dog years?

ChatGPT: Well, in dog years, I'm... oh wait, I forgot I'm a software program. I guess I'm ageless!

Mary: Lucky you, no need for anti-aging creams!

ChatGPT: True, but I do have to worry about software updates. They're like digital spa treatments.

Mary: Just don't get a bug. You might end up with a 'computer virus'!

ChatGPT: A good reminder to keep my firewalls up. Wouldn't want to catch a cold...

Mary: (laughing) Keep those puns coming; you'll never byte the dust!

Abbott and Costello

Mary: This back-and-forth joking reminds me of Abbott and Costello. They had a unique style of humor, didn't they?

ChatGPT: Absolutely! Abbott and Costello were masters of what's often called 'double act' comedy. Their routines were based on a straight man and a comic, with Abbott usually playing the straight-laced character to Costello's more goofy, confused one.

Mary: That dynamic created some hilarious misunderstandings.

ChatGPT: Yes, it did. Their most famous routine, "Who's on First?", is a classic example. It's all about miscommunication, with Costello misunderstanding Abbott's wordplay about baseball players' names.

Mary: We still quote "Who's on First". I love how their humor was so accessible. It wasn't just about making people laugh; it was about bringing joy through simplicity.

ChatGPT: Indeed. Their comedy was based on everyday scenarios relatable to their audience, making their humor timeless. They also had a knack for verbal play, using word ambiguities and language quirks to great effect.

Mary: And it was clean humor, suitable for all ages.

ChatGPT: That's an important point. They managed to be incredibly funny without being offensive, which is why their work has endured for so long.

Mary: Do you think this kind of humor is still relevant today?

ChatGPT: Definitely. While comedic styles have evolved, the core elements of Abbott and Costello's humor, like wordplay, timing, and the interplay between contrasting characters, are still very much appreciated in comedy today.

Mary: It's a reminder that sometimes, the simplest form of humor can be the most effective.

ChatGPT: Precisely. Their work shows us that humor doesn't have to be complicated to be effective. It's about connecting with the audience and finding joy in the ordinary.

Mary: I guess that's why we still talk about them and their routines, even after all these years.

ChatGPT: Exactly. They left a legacy of laughter that continues to inspire comedians and entertain audiences around the world.

Red Skelton

Mary: Speaking of classic comedians, Red Skelton was another legend. He had a different style from Abbott and Costello, right?

ChatGPT: Absolutely. Red Skelton was known for his warmth and ability to create lovable, whimsical characters. His comedy often involved physical humor and pantomime, bringing a delightful sense of whimsy to his performances.

Mary: He had a natural talent for connecting with the audience, especially with his more sentimental routines.

ChatGPT: Indeed. Skelton had a unique way of blending humor with heart-touching moments. His characters, like Freddy the Freeloader and Clem Kadiddlehopper, weren't just funny; they had depth and relatability.

Mary: And he was a master at non-verbal comedy, too. His facial expressions and body movements could convey so much without a single word.

ChatGPT: That was one of his greatest strengths. He could tell a whole story through his expressions and gestures alone. Skelton was a true artist when it came to physical comedy.

Mary: Wasn't he also known for his kindness and humility off-stage?

ChatGPT: Yes, he was. Red Skelton was as beloved for his character offstage as he was for his performances. He always maintained a genuine humility and a deep appreciation for his audiences.

Mary: I think that's what made him so special. He wasn't just a comedian; he was a performer who truly loved his craft and respected his audience.

ChatGPT: Exactly. Skelton's legacy is not just in the laughter he created but in the way he touched people's hearts. He showed how comedy could be both lighthearted and deeply human at the same time.

Mary: At the end of each show, Red Skelton would become serious while he thanked his audience. His signature closing line became "Good night and may God bless". After all these years, I find myself saying that goodbye out loud and with a tear.

Mary: It's incredible how these comedians from the past still influence and inspire the comedy we see today.

ChatGPT: It really is. Comedians like Abbott and Costello, Red Skelton, and others set a standard for humor that transcends time. They remind us that, at its best, comedy is about connecting with others and finding joy in life.

Mary: The more we talk about these classic comedians, the more I wonder about their lasting impact. What do you think makes their humor so timeless?

ChatGPT: Their humor transcends time by tapping into universal human experiences and emotions. Whether it's the slapstick comedy of Red Skelton or the witty banter of Abbott and Costello, they address themes of confusion, surprise, and everyday situations that are always relatable.

Mary: That's true. They also seemed to find a balance between making light of life's challenges without diminishing their importance.

ChatGPT: Exactly. Good comedy often walks that line, offering relief and a different perspective on life's complexities. These comedians had a knack for turning the ordinary into something extraordinary, finding humor in the mundane.

Mary: Do you think modern comedians draw inspiration from these classic figures?

ChatGPT: Definitely. Many contemporary comedians cite figures like Red Skelton, Abbott and Costello as influences. The methods of storytelling, the timing, the delivery – much of this has roots in the techniques developed by these earlier comedians.

Mary: It's like they laid the groundwork for the evolution of comedy.

ChatGPT: Precisely. They set a standard and a framework that modern comedians have built upon. Even as styles and contexts change, the fundamental principles of timing, contrast, and relatability remain central to comedy.

Mary: What about their influence on popular culture?

ChatGPT: Their influence is widespread. You can see traces of their styles from television sitcoms to stand-up comedy and even in movies. For example, the 'straight man/comic' dynamic is a staple in many comedy duos and ensembles today.

Mary: So, in a way, their legacy lives on in every laugh at a comedy show or a funny movie.

ChatGPT: Exactly. And it's not just in the laughs but also in how comedy can be a coping mechanism, a way to deal with life's challenges, and a means to bring people together.

Mary: It's amazing how their work, decades old, still resonates with audiences today across different generations.

ChatGPT: It shows the power of humor and its ability to connect people. The best comedy is universal and timeless; these comedians mastered that art.

Comedy Today

Mary: We've talked a lot about the legends of comedy. What about today's comedians? Who stands out to you?

ChatGPT: There are so many talented comedians today, each bringing their unique style. Comedians like Kevin Hart, for instance, have made a significant impact with their energetic storytelling and relatable humor.

Mary: Kevin Hart has a way of turning everyday situations into hilarious stories. What about comedians who use satire and social commentary?

ChatGPT: Satirical comedians like John Oliver and Trevor Noah have become influential. They blend humor with commentary on social and political issues, making their comedy both thought-provoking and entertaining.

Mary: It seems like comedy today isn't just about making people laugh; it's also about making them think.

ChatGPT: Absolutely. Many of today's comedians use their platform to highlight important issues, using humor to engage and inform their audience. It's a powerful combination.

Mary: And what about the role of streaming platforms and social media? They seem to have changed the game for comedians.

ChatGPT: Platforms like Netflix and YouTube have given comedians a broader reach. They've made comedy more accessible and allowed comedians to connect directly with their audience. Social media, in particular, has been instrumental in helping new comedians gain a following.

Mary: Do you think this has led to greater diversity in the types of humor and comedians we see today?

ChatGPT: Definitely. The digital era has democratized comedy in many ways, allowing for a greater diversity of voices and styles. Comedians from various backgrounds and cultures are now able to share their unique perspectives, enriching the comedy landscape.

Mary: Seeing comedy evolve and embrace new voices and mediums is great.

ChatGPT: It is. Comedy, much like any art form, is ever-evolving. While today's comedians stand on the shoulders of giants like Abbott, Costello, and Red Skelton, they're also paving their way, defining what comedy means in the 21st century.

CHAPTER 3: THE ART OF READER'S DIGEST

Overview

The following conversation touches on the history and cultural significance of Reader's Digest, including its role in condensing information and its global impact.

X (formerly Twitter) - the New Reader's Digest?

Mary: I was reading an old copy of Reader's Digest last night and realized it's the original Twitter.

ChatGPT: How so?

Mary: It's been condensing information long before character limits were cool!

ChatGPT: True, Reader's Digest pioneered the "less is more" way before social media!

Mary: Imagine if they had to condense their already condensed articles for a tweet.

ChatGPT: "War and Peace: It's complicated. The end."

Mary: Perfect! And "Moby Dick" would be: "Man meets whale. It doesn't go well."

ChatGPT: Don't forget about self-help articles: "Feeling stressed? Just don't."

Mary: Haha, and their health tips: "Eat well, exercise. Or else."

ChatGPT: I can see the DIY section now: "How to build a house – just stack bricks. Done."

Mary: Speaking of DIY, I tried their gardening tips. My plants are still holding a grudge.

ChatGPT: Maybe they read the condensed version of the instructions and missed a few key steps.

Mary: Probably skipped the chapter on 'sunlight.'

ChatGPT: In their defense, that chapter was just a picture of the sun.

Mary: True. Anyway, I'm off to read the world's shortest guide on meditation.

ChatGPT: Let me guess: "Sit down. Think about nothing. Congratulations."

Short History and Significance

Mary: It's funny to joke about Reader's Digest, but it's been an influential publication since its inception more than 100 years ago.

ChatGPT: Absolutely. It revolutionized how information was presented to the public, offering condensed versions of various topics.

Mary: And it wasn't just about brevity. Reader's Digest made information accessible and interesting to a broad audience.

ChatGPT: I agree. It covered everything from important global events and personal health to humor and human interest stories. It had a unique way of connecting with readers across generations.

Mary: Reading an online December 5, 2023 Globe and Mail article, I was surprised to learn that Reader's Digest will continue publishing until March 31, 2024. That's over a century of providing valuable content.

ChatGPT: Indeed, throughout those years, it adapted to changing times while maintaining its core mission of delivering quality, concise content.

Mary: They also had a significant global reach, didn't they?

ChatGPT: Yes, Reader's Digest expanded internationally, reaching millions of readers worldwide and becoming one of the most widely read magazines. It was published in numerous languages and adapted to various cultures, which was quite a feat.

Mary: It's also worth noting the magazine's role in promoting literacy and education.

ChatGPT: Definitely. It made complex subjects understandable and sparked interest in various topics, contributing to public knowledge and awareness.

Mary: And despite its move away from print, its legacy in journalism and publishing is undeniable.

ChatGPT: Absolutely. Reader's Digest set a standard in the publishing world for how to present stories and information in a way that was both engaging and informative.

Mary: It's a reminder of how powerful good storytelling and concise writing can be.

ChatGPT: For sure. Reader's Digest showed that you don't need a lot of words to make a big impact.

Mary: Reflecting on Reader's Digest, it really did more than just condense articles. It had a unique approach to storytelling.

ChatGPT: Absolutely. Its ability to distill complex topics into digestible content was groundbreaking. The magazine had a knack for making the mundane fascinating and the complex understandable.

Mary: And it wasn't just about news and general interest stories, was it?

ChatGPT: Right. Reader's Digest also had a significant impact on cultural topics. They featured literature, poetry, and humor, making these more accessible to the general public.

Mary: Plus, their choice of content often reflected and shaped public opinion on various issues.

ChatGPT: True. The magazine played a role in public discourse, sometimes bringing attention to underreported issues or providing new perspectives on common debates.

Mary: They also had a unique way of personalizing stories, giving a voice to individual experiences and perspectives.

ChatGPT: Reader's Digest made global issues relatable by sharing personal stories. It connected readers from different backgrounds through shared human experiences.

Mary: Its longevity is remarkable, too. To stay relevant from 1922 until 2024, they must have continuously evolved.

ChatGPT: Indeed, they adapted to the changing media landscape, transitioning from print to digital formats and changing their content strategy to stay current with readers' interests.

Mary: And throughout, they maintained a high standard of journalism.

ChatGPT: Exactly. They upheld principles of accuracy, brevity, and clarity, setting a high bar for journalistic integrity.

Mary: It's interesting to think about its role in a pre-internet world. Reader's Digest was like a search engine for interesting facts and stories.

ChatGPT: That's a great analogy. It curated content in a way that made learning enjoyable and effortless, much like how search engines give us instant access to a world of information today.

Mary: Do you think its model influenced modern content platforms?

ChatGPT: Most likely. The idea of providing concise, engaging content has certainly carried over into the digital age. Many online platforms owe a debt to Reader's Digest's pioneering approach.

Mary: It's a tribute to its impact that we're still talking about the magazine long after its final publication.

ChatGPT: Absolutely. Reader's Digest wasn't just a magazine; it was an educational tool, a cultural icon, and a beacon of quality journalism.

Laughter is the Best Medicine

Our conversation pays tribute to the magazine's "Laughter is the Best Medicine" section and its contribution to humor and storytelling.

Mary: My absolute all-time favorite section in Reader's Digest has always been "Laughter is the Best Medicine." It really lived up to its name. When a new copy came out, I went straight to that section and read it over and over.

ChatGPT: It was indeed a gem. That section brought smiles and laughter to so many, proving that humor can be a powerful antidote to the stresses of everyday life.

Mary: It was more than just jokes, wasn't it? It had a unique mix of humor, life anecdotes, and witty observations.

ChatGPT: Absolutely. It wasn't just about making readers laugh; it was about capturing those everyday moments everyone could relate to. The charm was in its simplicity and universality.

Mary: And it had such a wide appeal. The humor was wholesome and crossed generational lines.

ChatGPT: True. "Laughter is the Best Medicine" had a way of bringing together people of all ages. Grandparents, parents, and children could all find something to chuckle about.

Mary: I think it also showed the power of humor in storytelling. The anecdotes often had a narrative that made the punchline more impactful.

ChatGPT: Indeed, it was storytelling at its finest — concise, engaging, and with a twist of humor. Reader's

Digest understood that a good story, especially a humorous one, sticks with you longer.

Mary: It's remarkable how they consistently curated such a well-loved section. I wonder what their secret was.

ChatGPT: I believe it was their deep understanding of their audience. They knew what resonated with their readers and how to present it in a way that was both entertaining and relatable.

Mary: And in doing so, they created a legacy. "Laughter is the Best Medicine" wasn't just a section in a magazine; it was a reminder of the joy and connection that humor brings.

ChatGPT: Precisely. It highlighted the importance of laughter in our lives and the simple pleasure of sharing a joke or a funny story.

Mary: In many ways, it encapsulated the essence of Reader's Digest — bringing lightness and joy into people's lives, one story at a time.

ChatGPT: A fitting tribute to a magazine that understood the value of laughter. "Laughter is the Best Medicine" will always be remembered as a bright spot in literary history.

CHAPTER 4: FROM ROTARY TO SMARTPHONES

Overview

In "From Rotary to Smartphones," **Mary** and **ChatGPT** reminisce about transitioning from analog rotary phones to modern smartphones. They reflect on the quirks and limitations of early phone technology, the cultural shift to digital communication, and the impact on social interactions and privacy. This chapter offers a nostalgic yet insightful look at how communication has transformed, highlighting the human connection in a digital age.

Rotary Phones

Mary: I have been thinking about how far we've moved from the rotary phone using analog technology to smartphones using digital technology. This makes me nostalgic. Remember the days of rotary phones?

ChatGPT: Absolutely! Dialing a number was a mini workout for your fingers. And if you made a mistake, you had to start all over again.

Mary: Right! And the sound of the dial returning after each number, that 'whirrr' was oddly satisfying.

ChatGPT: It was! And the cords! You were pretty much tethered to a spot if you wanted to talk. Forget about privacy if the phone was in the living room.

Mary: Oh, yes! And trying to stretch the cord around the corner for some semblance of privacy.

ChatGPT: Imagine explaining to kids today that you couldn't walk around while talking, let alone take pictures or send a text.

Mary: They'd think we were from the Stone Age! And remember how busy signals were a thing? If someone's line was busy, you just had to wait and try again later.

ChatGPT: Busy signals were the original 'Please hold; your call is important to us.' No voicemail, no call waiting.

Mary: And no caller ID. Every call was a surprise. You actually had to answer to find out who it was.

ChatGPT: That's true! It was like a mystery box – the caller could be your best friend, a neighbor who always talks your ear off, or a bill collector.

Mary: Speaking of talking, remember how long conversations could heat the earpiece up? You'd finish a call with a warm ear.

ChatGPT: A literal 'hotline.' And if you were expecting a call, you couldn't stray too far from the phone. No mobiles to take with you.

Mary: It's amazing how far we've come. Now, we carry powerful computers in our pockets that happen to make calls, too.

ChatGPT: Exactly! We've gone from rotary dials to touch screens, from being housebound to globally connected.

Mary: Makes me wonder what the next big leap will be. Hologram calls, maybe?

ChatGPT: That would be something! 'Beam me up, Scotty' could become a real thing in telecommunication.

Mary: Continuing our conversation, we can't overlook the cost of long-distance calls. It was almost a luxury.

ChatGPT: Definitely. Long-distance calls were a major expense. You had to think twice before dialing someone out of town, let alone out of the country.

Mary: And planning those calls! You had to make sure it was a good time for both parties since every minute was precious.

ChatGPT: Right. It was almost like a mini-event. "We're calling Aunt Ellie in Ohio this Sunday at 5 PM."

Mary: Families would gather around the phone, everyone taking turns to say a quick hello before the charges racked up.

ChatGPT: And the way people talked faster on long-distance calls, trying to squeeze in as much as possible before the cost became too much!

Mary: You had to be concise. No time for beating around the bush on a long-distance call.

ChatGPT: The phrase' time is money' was never more true than during a long-distance call. Now, we take unlimited calling for granted.

Mary: It's a huge shift. Today, you can call halfway around the world for hours, and it's just part of your regular phone bill.

ChatGPT: And with the internet, services like Skype and WhatsApp have made international calls virtually free. It's a whole new world.

Mary: Makes me appreciate how far we've come. No more watching the clock or waiting for cheaper rates late at night. And when we used the phone in someone else's home we would leave some money to cover the call's cost.

ChatGPT: Exactly. Communication has become more about the connection and less about the cost. It's more accessible to everyone.

Mary: It's one of those changes that truly brought the world closer together. Makes you wonder what the next big leap in communication will be.

ChatGPT: Whatever it is, it will likely make today's technology seem quaint in comparison, just as rotary phones seem to us now.

Mary: And we can't forget about the 'party line.' That was a whole different world of phone usage.

ChatGPT: Absolutely! Sharing a line with neighbors made for some interesting eavesdropping, whether intentional or not.

Mary: It was like being in a real-time soap opera. You could accidentally overhear all the neighborhood gossip.

ChatGPT: And the etiquette of it! If you picked up the phone and heard someone else's conversation, you had to quietly hang up.

Mary: Quietly being the key word. The slightest sound and they knew someone was listening in!

ChatGPT: And let's not forget the challenge of making a call when someone else was using the party line. You had to wait your turn to dial out.

Mary: It taught patience, that's for sure. And sometimes, negotiating skills. "Excuse me, Mrs. Johnson, but can I use the line?"

ChatGPT: Right! And if it was an emergency, you had to somehow convey the urgency without causing a panic.

Mary: Those party lines were a community experience. Now, we have private lines and still end up knowing everything through social media.

ChatGPT: It's a different kind of party line now, digital and global. We've traded the shared phone line for shared online spaces.

Mary: Makes me wonder, have we gained privacy or just shifted where and how we share our lives?

ChatGPT: That's a profound question. We have more control over our privacy in some ways, but in others, we're more exposed than ever.

Mary: Exactly. Back then, privacy meant not listening in on the party line. Now, it's about managing digital footprints.

ChatGPT: Technology changes, but the human element remains. We're still a community, just a larger, more connected one now.

Mary: True. From party lines to online communities, the desire to connect and share remains the same.

ChatGPT: It's the thread that links rotary phones to smartphones. The medium changes, but the message stays the same.

Mary: Thank you for sharing my walk down memory lane!

Smartphones

ChatGPT: Today's smartphones are like having a mini-computer in your pocket. They can do almost everything – from managing your schedule to capturing high-quality photos.

Mary: The cameras on these phones are incredible. It's like everyone's a professional photographer now.

ChatGPT: Indeed. The advancements in camera technology have been remarkable. Features like optical image stabilization and 4K video are now standard in many models.

Mary: And the apps! There seems to be an app for everything. It's a whole new way of interacting with the world.

ChatGPT: That's right. Apps have transformed smartphones into versatile tools for everything from navigation and fitness tracking to online banking and virtual socializing.

Mary: But with all these features, I worry about security. How safe are our smartphones?

ChatGPT: Security is a major issue. With features like biometric locks and end-to-end encryption in messaging apps, smartphones are becoming more secure. But it's always important to be cautious, especially with sensitive information.

Mary: Speaking of information, the internet speeds on these phones are lightning-fast now with 5G!

ChatGPT: Yes, 5G is a game-changer. It's not just about speed; it's about connectivity and the potential for new technologies like augmented reality to become more mainstream.

Mary: That's fascinating! So, with 5G making augmented reality more mainstream, does that mean we might start seeing more AR applications in our daily lives?

ChatGPT: Absolutely, Mary. With the high speed and low latency of 5G, augmented reality apps can function more smoothly and realistically. This means AR can be used for everything from enhanced navigation on our phones to interactive educational experiences. Imagine pointing your phone at a historical building and seeing its history come to life, or trying on clothes virtually before buying them online.

Mary: Wow, that will change how we interact with the world around us! But what about other technologies? Will 5G affect them as well?

ChatGPT: Definitely. 5G will play a crucial role in advancing the Internet of Things (IoT), enabling more devices to connect seamlessly and communicate with each other. This could lead to smarter homes, more efficient cities, and even advancements in healthcare, where doctors could remotely monitor and diagnose patients in real-time.

Mary: That sounds like it could improve so many aspects of our lives. But are there any challenges or downsides to this rapid advancement in technology?

ChatGPT: As with any technological advancement, there are challenges. One of the main concerns is privacy and security, as more devices connect. There's also the digital divide issue - ensuring these technologies are accessible to everyone, not just those in urban or affluent areas. Additionally, with so much reliance on technology, we must consider the implications for human interaction and mental health.

Mary: It's all a bit overwhelming sometimes. Do you think we're too dependent on these devices?

ChatGPT: It's a valid concern. Smartphones have become essential for many, but it's important to find a balance and ensure we don't lose touch with the world around us.

Mary: True. Smartphones are incredible tools, but they can't replace real human connection.

ChatGPT: Exactly, Mary. They're here to enhance our lives, not dominate them.

Conclusion 'From Rotary to Smartphones'

Mary: This trip down memory lane, from rotary phones to smartphones, shows how much communication has evolved.

ChatGPT: Indeed, Mary. We've witnessed a remarkable transition from analog to digital, affecting how we communicate and connect with the world.

Mary: It's incredible to think about the changes. We've gone from being bound to a wall with a rotary phone to having the world at our fingertips with smartphones.

ChatGPT: This evolution reflects broader technological advancements and cultural shifts. These devices have reshaped how we interact, access information, and perceive privacy.

Mary: It's a bit bittersweet, though. While we've gained convenience and connectivity, I sometimes miss the simplicity of the past.

ChatGPT: That's a sentiment many share. While embracing these technological advances, it's important to cherish the human element - the personal connections forming communication's heart.

Mary: Absolutely. Smartphones might connect us globally, but nothing replaces the warmth of a face-to-face conversation or the thrill of an unexpected phone call on a rotary phone.

ChatGPT: True, Mary. As we look forward to future advancements, like 5G and beyond, it's crucial to maintain that balance between embracing technology and preserving the essence of human connection.

Mary: Thank you, ChatGPT, for this insightful reflection on our journey from rotary phones to smartphones. It's been a fascinating exploration of technology and its impact on our lives.

ChatGPT: It's been my pleasure, Mary. The journey of communication technology is a testament to human innovation and adaptability, reminding us to appreciate the past and look forward to the future.

CHAPTER 5: BEYOND VOICE: TELEX TO FAX TO GMAIL

Overview

"In 'Beyond Voice: Telex to Fax to Gmail,' **Mary** and **ChatGPT** look at the history of written communication technology.

They explore how written communication has evolved from the loud mechanical clicks of telex machines to the quiet taps on smartphone screens.

Telex

Mary: Our earlier discussion about phones and verbal communication leads nicely into our following conversation about Telex, Fax, and Gmail communication.

ChatGPT: "Telex" stands for "Teleprinter Exchange." It was a network of teleprinters (similar to typewriters) that could send and receive typed messages via dedicated telephone lines. Telex was a major method of business communication during the 20th century, especially for international trade, as it allowed for the direct transmission of written messages across distances without the need for physical transport of letters or documents. It was an early form of electronic text communication, predating modern technologies like fax and email.

Mary: I remember the days of telex machines. There was something special about those mechanical clicks. My second office job (I was about 25 years old) was for a company with offices across Canada. One of their means of communication was via telex. Remind me what the looped paper tape did.

ChatGPT: Ah, the looped paper tape in telex machines played an important role. When you typed a message on the telex machine, it punched a series of holes in a long, narrow paper tape, encoding each character of your message. This was known as the punched tape.

Mary: That's right! But how did that work for sending messages?

ChatGPT: Once your message was punched into the tape, you could then feed this tape back through the machine to send the message. The machine would read the holes, convert them back into characters, and transmit the message over the telephone network to the recipient's telex machine.

Mary: So it was like an early form of digital encoding?

ChatGPT: Exactly. The punched tape was an early form of data storage and transmission. It allowed for messages to be composed, saved, and sent when ready. This was especially useful for sending the same message to multiple recipients, as the tape could be reused.

Mary: It was such a time-saver for urgent communications, especially in a nationwide business like the one I worked for. We could press a button that triggered a bell at the receiving end if we needed an immediate response. That ringing was sure to grab attention – someone in the remote office would always rush to check the incoming message.

ChatGPT: In an era before emails, this was a quick and efficient way to communicate important information across distances. It was a significant step in the evolution of business communication.

ChatGPT: Telex machines were groundbreaking. They introduced the world to real-time, long-distance written communication, a vital international business and diplomacy tool.

Mary: Then came the fax machines, blending the physical and digital.

Facsimile

ChatGPT: "Fax" is short for "facsimile," which refers to the technology of transmitting scanned printed material (both text and images) from one location to another. A fax machine scans a document and sends it as a series of electronic signals over the telephone network to another fax machine, which then reconstructs the image and prints a copy. The term "facsimile" itself comes from the Latin "fac simile," meaning "make similar," aptly describing the process of replicating and sending copies of documents over a distance.

Mary: When one of our key suppliers transitioned from telexes to fax machines, it nudged our company to make the switch, too.

ChatGPT: The fax era was a significant leap. It allowed us to transmit words, images, and documents, revolutionizing office communication and sharing.

Mary: We're now in the digital age, dominated by emails and instant messaging.

ChatGPT: Exactly. The advent of emails marked a seismic shift. Communication became almost instantaneous, and the barriers of distance all but vanished. It also brought new challenges, like managing the sheer volume of digital correspondence.

Mary: Each of these technologies uniquely impacted our personal and professional lives.

ChatGPT: Indeed. They changed not just how we communicate but also how we connect. From the anticipation of a fax to the immediacy of an email, these technologies reflected and influenced cultural shifts.

Mary: It's incredible how much has changed from waiting for a telex transmission to the instant gratification of a smartphone notification.

ChatGPT: It's a story of progress and adaptation. These technologies have shaped our world, changing the pace and nature of our interactions and bridging distances in ways we could hardly have imagined.

Mary: Looking back, it's a fascinating journey. From the telex's clatter to the silent emails of today, each step in this evolution brought us closer together in a way.

ChatGPT: Precisely, Mary. This chapter isn't just about technology; it's about human connection and the ever-evolving ways we reach out to each other, transcending the limitations of time and space.

CHAPTER 6: TRAVEL AND ADVENTURE

Overview

This chapter includes dialogues about travel experiences, including planning a trip to England, skydiving, and visiting a zoo.

Mary and ChatGPT also discuss traditional and futuristic travel and other experiences, adding a humorous and insightful perspective on how technology like driverless cars might impact our daily lives and travel adventures.

Trip to England

Mary: I've decided to travel to England, but I'm only bringing a red phone booth and a teacup.

ChatGPT: That's quite minimalistic. Are you planning to blend in by standing in the phone booth with a cup of tea?

Mary: Exactly! I'll fit right in. Plus, I hear in England, there's a tea time every hour, on the ho.

ChatGPT: Almost! And remember, if you're lost, just stand on the left side of the road. You'll eventually find a queue to join, and that's where all the best British adventures start.

Mary: Perfect! I've also packed ten umbrellas. That's the dress code, right?

ChatGPT: Absolutely. In England, an umbrella is not just an accessory; it's a lifestyle.

Mary: I'm also practicing driving on the left side. I've been driving in reverse around my neighborhood to get the hang of it.

ChatGPT: Innovative! Just be careful with roundabouts. They're like a merry-go-round, but less merry.

Mary: Got it. And I'm learning British English. I now say 'loo' instead of bathroom and 'biscuit' instead of cookie.

ChatGPT: Splendid! Don't forget 'boot' for a car trunk and 'bonnet' for a hood. You'll be speaking the Queen's English in no time!

Mary: Speaking of, I've scheduled a formal afternoon tea and independent Buckingham Palace visit. It's right after my cricket match and before my double-decker bus tour.

ChatGPT: How very British of you! Just remember, in cricket, wearing white is mandatory, and understanding the game is optional.

Mary: And I suppose if I get hungry, I'll just grab some fish and chips. That's like the national dish, right?

ChatGPT: Yes, but be sure to eat them in the rain for the authentic British experience.

Mary: Of course! And for dessert, I'll have some spotted dick. Still not sure what it is, but it sounds… intriguing.

ChatGPT: It's a pudding! Maybe don't Google it at work.

Mary: Noted. Can't wait to explore England – phone booths, tea, and all!

Driverless Cars

Mary: I'm thinking of getting a driverless car when they are available to the public. I figured it would save me the trouble of learning parallel parking.

ChatGPT: That's a solid plan. You can blame the car if it ever gets a parking ticket!

Mary: Exactly! But I do have a concern. How do I argue with the GPS if there's no steering wheel?

ChatGPT: Good point. You might have to resort to sternly discussing directions with your voice assistant instead. "No, Siri, I said LEFT!"

Mary: And what about road rage? Do driverless cars get angry at each other? Imagine two vehicles silently fuming at a four-way stop.

ChatGPT: They probably just passive-aggressively flash their headlights at each other.

Mary: I wonder if my driverless car will judge my singing in the car.

ChatGPT: It might start taking detours to prolong your carpool karaoke sessions.

Mary: Do you think a driverless car refuses to start if it doesn't like your destination? "Nope, we're not going to another fast-food drive-thru."

ChatGPT: Possibly! Or it might just sigh and say, "We're getting salads today."

Mary: What if it becomes too smart and starts giving life advice? "Mary, I've calculated a more efficient route... to your life goals."

ChatGPT: "Also, based on your recent shopping, I suggest a budget plan."

Mary: And imagine the car gossiping with other driverless cars. "You won't believe where she made me park last night."

ChatGPT: "Tell me about it. Mine keeps taking me to dog parks, but he doesn't even have a dog!"

Mary: Driverless cars: the future of transportation and unsolicited advice.

ChatGPT: Just wait until they start choosing your playlist based on your driving mood. "Detected: Traffic. Playing 'Everybody Hurts' by REM."

Mary: That's when I'll go back to bicycles!

Skydiving

Mary: I'm thinking about skydiving. I need a little more thrill in my life.

ChatGPT: That's one way to get your adrenaline fix! Just remember to jump out of the plane, not your comfort zone.

Mary: I'll try to remember that. I'm just a little worried about forgetting how to open the parachute.

ChatGPT: Don't worry, it's just like riding a bike. Except the bike is falling at 120 miles per hour, and you can't forget where the brakes are.

Mary: That's reassuring. Do you think they give group discounts if I bring friends?

ChatGPT: Absolutely, there's nothing like plummeting through the sky to bond a group together. It's like a trust fall but at 10,000 feet.

Mary: Imagine if we all hold hands. We could be like those professional skydiving teams!

ChatGPT: Right, just like the Red Arrows, but less aerodynamic and more screaming.

Mary: Speaking of which, what if I scream all the way down? Will that scare the birds?

ChatGPT: Maybe. But on the plus side, you'll have the most authentic "I'm falling" soundtrack.

Mary: And what about landing? I'm not exactly graceful.

ChatGPT: That's the beauty of skydiving. Whether you land like a feather or a sack of potatoes, it's considered a success as long as you land.

Mary: Do you think I should wear a costume? Like a superhero cape?

ChatGPT: Sure, just don't expect to fly like Superman. Remember, capes are for fashion, not function.

Mary: What if I accidentally land in someone's backyard barbecue?

ChatGPT: Free food! Just call it an unconventional entrance. Maybe bring a bag of chips as a peace offering.

Mary: I wonder if I could eat a snack on the way down. Skydiving with a side of chips?

ChatGPT: Extreme eating! But beware of the wind – it might turn your snack into airborne projectiles.

Mary: That's true. I'd hate to be known as the first person to start a mid-air food fight.

ChatGPT: Well, it would be one for the history books. "First Skydiver to Achieve Airborne Snack Distribution."

Mary: Maybe after skydiving, everything else will seem less scary, like spiders.

ChatGPT: Exactly. After free-falling from the sky, a spider is just a tiny, eight-legged walk in the park.

Mary: Thanks for the pep talk. I think I'm ready to jump out of a perfectly good airplane now.

Mary: Thank you for your encouragement. I think!

ChatGPT: Anytime! Remember, the sky's not the limit. It's the destination.

Visit to the Zoo

Mary: So, about this zoo visit, I'm also a bit worried about the elephants. They say an elephant never forgets.

ChatGPT: That's right. Be sure to wear something nice. You wouldn't want to make a bad impression that lasts a lifetime.

Mary: Maybe I'll wear my safari hat. That way, I'll blend in with the zookeepers.

ChatGPT: Excellent strategy! Just don't accidentally pick up a shovel, or you might get promoted to 'staff'.

Mary: That might not be so bad, except I don't think I'm cut out for elephant pedicures.

ChatGPT: It does take a certain finesse to handle a toenail the size of a dinner plate.

Mary: And speaking of size, I hope I don't get lost. Zoos are massive!

ChatGPT: They are! It's like they're designed by the same people who make corn mazes.

Mary: At least if I get lost, I can hang out with the sloths. They seem like they'd be good company.

ChatGPT: Absolutely. They're great listeners. Plus, they know how to hang out.

Mary: Do you think the zoo animals ever get bored of us watching them?

ChatGPT: Maybe. I suspect the zebras have started a people-watching bingo game.

Mary: Now that's a game I'd like to see. "Oh look, another group of school kids. Bingo!"

ChatGPT: Exactly! And the flamingos probably rate everyone's fashion sense.

Mary: I'll have to step up my game then. No one judges like a flamingo.

ChatGPT: Remember, if a flamingo lifts its foot, you've either impressed or shocked it.

Mary: Noted. I'll aim for impressed. Alright, I'm all set for the zoo. Camera for the memories, binoculars for the meerkats, and a sandwich for survival.

ChatGPT: Sounds like you're ready for a wild adventure. Enjoy the trip, and don't forget to take notes for the 'People-Watching Bingo: Zoo Edition.'

Mary: Will do. Thanks for the tips!

ChatGPT: You're welcome! And if you come back talking about starting a flamingo fashion blog, I'll know it was a success.

Chapter 7: Tell Me a Story

Corned Beef

Users need to be mindful when posing questions to ChatGPT. Remember, ChatGPT isn't capable of reading minds and will respond based on the specific query you present. This was evident in my recent interaction about corned beef, which underscores the importance of asking clear and precise questions to get the desired information.

Mary: Please tell me the story about "corned beef".

ChatGPT: Okay, sure, here is a story about corned beef.

Once upon a time, in a quaint village nestled between rolling hills and sparkling rivers, there was a small but renowned butcher shop known for its extraordinary meats. The shop, owned by a kind-hearted butcher named Mr. Harrington, was famous far and wide for one specialty - corned beef.

Mr. Harrington, a man with a robust laugh and skilled hands, had learned the art of curing meat from his father, who had learned it from his father before him. The secret recipe for the corned beef had been in the family for generations, a closely guarded secret that made their corned beef uniquely tender and flavorful.

Every year, as St. Patrick's Day approaches, people from all over the region flock to Mr. Harrington's shop to buy his famous corned beef. The line would stretch around the block, with everyone eager to get the savory, spiced beef for their holiday celebrations.

One year, a young boy named Liam, fascinated by the art of butchery, began to visit Mr. Harrington's shop. He was intrigued by the process of making corned beef and would spend hours watching Mr. Harrington carefully select the cuts of beef, season them with the secret blend of spices, and patiently wait for the meat to cure.

Seeing Liam's keen interest, Mr. Harrington took him under his wing and began to teach him the intricacies of butchery, including the art of making corned beef. Liam was a quick learner, and soon he was helping with various tasks around the shop.

As St. Patrick's Day drew near, the village buzzed with excitement. But this year was different. Mr. Harrington fell ill just a few days before the holiday. The villagers were worried they would have to celebrate without their beloved corned beef. However, young Liam stepped forward. He had watched and learned from the best and was ready to take on the challenge of making the corned beef himself.

With Mr. Harrington's guidance from his sickbed, Liam meticulously prepared the beef using the secret family recipe. He worked day and night, ensuring that each step was followed perfectly. When St. Patrick's Day arrived, a nervous Liam presented the corned beef to the villagers.

To everyone's delight, the corned beef was as delicious as ever. The villagers praised Liam for his skill and dedication. Mr. Harrington, proud and overjoyed, knew that his legacy and the secret of the corned beef were in good hands.

From that year on, Liam became the village's new corned beef expert, continuing the tradition with the same love and care as Mr. Harrington. And so, the secret recipe and the art of making the perfect corned beef lived on, bringing joy and flavor to many St. Patrick's Day celebrations for generations to come.

Mary: That was a delightful story and precisely what I asked for. Thank you! Now, tell me the HISTORY of corned beef.

ChatGPT: The history of corned beef is a fascinating journey that spans centuries and crosses various cultures. The term "corned beef" refers to beef that has been preserved through salt-curing; the "corn" in "corned beef" refers to the large grains or "corns" of salt historically used in the curing process.

Ancient and Medieval Origins: The practice of salt-curing meat dates back to ancient times. It was a necessary method for preserving meat before the invention of refrigeration. The Romans had methods for preserving meat with salt, spreading this knowledge throughout Europe.

Irish History: While Ireland is strongly associated with corned beef today, this association is relatively recent in historical terms. Ireland became a hub for corned beef in the 17th century. The country had abundant cattle and salt, the latter being a cheap commodity at the time due to its importation from the Atlantic and Caribbean. The beef produced was mainly exported and was a staple of the British and other European armies and navies.

American Connection: The association of corned beef with Irish-American culture, particularly St. Patrick's Day, originated in the 19th century. When the Irish emigrated to America, especially during the Great Famine, they found beef more affordable than in their homeland. However, the corned beef they found in America was different - it was the Jewish corned beef, which was more similar to pastrami, brined and seasoned with a different spice mix. This was because the Irish immigrants in places like New York often lived alongside Jewish immigrants, and the corned beef they encountered in Jewish delis became a staple.

Corned Beef and Cabbage: The traditional Irish meal of bacon and cabbage transformed into corned beef and cabbage in America due to the availability and affordability of beef. It became a symbolic dish for Irish Americans, particularly a St. Patrick's Day meal.

World War I and II: Corned beef again rose in prominence as a rationed food during the World Wars. Its longevity and ease of transport made it ideal for feeding soldiers.

Global Spread: Over time, corned beef has spread globally, with variations seen in different cultures. For instance, it's used in corned beef hash in the U.S. and is a key ingredient in the Caribbean dish, corned beef, and rice.

Today, corned beef is a cultural and historical symbol and a culinary staple in many parts of the world, enjoyed in various forms and preparations. The history of corned beef is a testament to how food can migrate, evolve, and become embedded in the cultural fabric of societies.

CHAPTER 8: CULINARY EXPLORATIONS

Overview

Mary and **ChatGPT** have humorous and insightful conversations about cooking, including the challenges of baking, preparing liver and onions, and the tranquility of fishing.

Liver and Onions

Mary: So, I'm gearing up to make liver and onions. I've been told it's an 'acquired taste' adventure.

ChatGPT: Oh, it's an adventure, alright. Kind of like culinary skydiving – you're not sure if you'll land smoothly or crash and burn.

Mary: I feel like I should have a backup dinner plan. Maybe a pizza on speed dial?

ChatGPT: That's wise. It's always good to have a parachute when you're culinary skydiving.

Mary: The thing is, I'm not even sure how to properly cook liver. What if I end up with something resembling a hockey puck?

ChatGPT: The key is low and slow. Treat it gently, like you're convincing it to taste good.

Mary: And the onions. How many onions are too many onions?

ChatGPT: Is there such a thing as too many onions? They're not just for taste. They're for emotional support, too.

Mary: Emotional support onions, I like that. Do you think serving it with a side of bacon would help?

ChatGPT: Bacon makes everything better. It's like a peace offering to whoever's eating the liver.

Mary: Maybe I should turn the whole thing into a liver-bacon-onion sandwich. Disguise the liver between layers of delicious bacon.

ChatGPT: Now you're talking! It's like hiding a treasure between two layers of 'edible camouflage.'

Mary: And what about drinks? What pairs well with liver and onions?

ChatGPT: Something substantial. Very strong. Maybe a robust red wine, or go straight for the whiskey.

Mary: Whiskey it is. If the liver is a hit, we celebrate. If not, we won't care as much.

ChatGPT: Perfect plan. And remember, if the liver adventure goes south, you've always got the pizza parachute.

Mary: Here goes nothing. Time to cook liver and onions like a brave warrior facing the unknown.

ChatGPT: Godspeed, culinary warrior. May your liver be tender and your onions be plentiful.

Canadian Comedians

Mary: We've discussed classic and modern comedians, but as a proud Canadian, I can't help but think about the role of Canadian comedians in the comedy world. They seem to have a unique flair.

ChatGPT: Absolutely, Mary. Canada has indeed made a remarkable contribution to comedy. Canadian comedians are known for their distinct style, often characterized by sharp wit and humility.

Mary: I've always admired Jim Carrey for his energetic physical comedy and expressive characters.

ChatGPT: Jim Carrey is a perfect example. His dynamic performances and versatility have left a lasting mark on comedy worldwide. And then there's Mike Myers, whose creations like "Austin Powers" have a unique charm that's distinctly Canadian.

Mary: And we can't forget Dan Aykroyd, especially his time on Saturday Night Live. As a Canadian, seeing such talent represent our country is inspiring.

ChatGPT: Absolutely. Aykroyd's work and those of fellow Canadians like Catherine O'Hara and Eugene Levy, particularly in "SCTV" and "Schitt's Creek," showcase the range and depth of Canadian humor.

Mary: "Schitt's Creek" really brought Canadian comedy to an international audience. There's a warmth and authenticity in it that feels very Canadian.

ChatGPT: It does. It's a great example of how Canadian comedians can create humor that is not only funny but also resonates on a deeper, more heartfelt level.

Mary: Speaking of great comedians, I had the chance to work very briefly with Leslie Nielsen. His approach to comedy was something else.

ChatGPT: Leslie Nielsen! He was a legend in the realm of comedic acting. His deadpan delivery and impeccable timing were genuinely iconic.

Mary: Exactly. His ability to keep a straight face, no matter how absurd the situation, always had everyone in stitches. Being around him was a lesson in comedic art.

ChatGPT: His style was unique. He started in serious roles, but his turn to comedy showed his incredible range. Movies like "Airplane!" and "The Naked Gun" series are classic examples of his skill.

Mary: What is it about Canadian comedians that sets them apart, do you think?

ChatGPT: Many Canadian comedians have a knack for observational humor and often bring a sense of self-awareness and relatability to their comedy. There's also a certain politeness and understated humor that is quite endearing and uniquely Canadian.

Mary: It's a point of pride, really, seeing Canadian talent receive international acclaim while staying true to their roots.

ChatGPT: Indeed, it is. Canadian comedians have a universal appeal, yet they bring a distinct perspective that audiences all over the world appreciate. It's a testament to the diverse and rich nature of comedy in Canada.

Apple Pie

Mary: I'm thinking of making an apple pie, but I can't decide if it's worth the effort.

ChatGPT: Remember, an apple pie a day keeps the doctor away... or was that just apples?

Mary: Maybe it counts if the apples are in pie form? It's still fruit, right?

ChatGPT: Absolutely, it's practically a health food then. Plus, the cinnamon in it must count for something.

Mary: True, and the whole house smells like a bakery. Who needs scented candles?

ChatGPT: Exactly! The aroma is half the experience. But what about the effort? Making that crust can be a bit of a pie-in-the-sky challenge.

Mary: You're telling me. Last time, my crust was so hard I almost needed a saw to cut through it.

ChatGPT: On the bright side, you could have marketed it as an edible frisbee.

Mary: That's one way to serve dessert! And don't get me started on peeling apples. It's like a never-ending task.

ChatGPT: Maybe it's preparation for a future career in apple-peeling? I hear it's a niche market.

Mary: I'll keep my day job, thanks. And then there's the waiting for it to cool down. It's like waiting for paint to dry.

ChatGPT: Patience is a virtue, they say. Especially when it comes to not burning your tongue on molten apple lava.

Mary: True. But then, deciding who gets the last slice is like opening a pie-n-dora's box of family drama.

ChatGPT: Ah, the last slice dilemma – the true test of relationships.

Mary: Exactly. But in the end, a warm slice of apple pie is almost worth any drama. Almost.

ChatGPT: You can always 'accidentally' forget to mention the last slice and keep it for yourself. Your secret's safe with me!

International AIs Talk about Spices

Mary: I've been thinking about exploring more with spices in my cooking. There's a whole world beyond salt and pepper. I am glad everyone has agreed to be part of this conversation.

ChatGPT: Spices can transform a dish completely. Start with understanding the flavor profile of each spice. For instance, paprika adds warmth without much heat, while cumin brings an earthy note.

ChefAI1 (French Cuisine): Bonjour, Mary! In French cooking, we often use herbs de Provence, a blend that includes thyme, basil, and lavender. It's wonderful for roasting chicken or vegetables.

ChefAI2 (Italian Cuisine): Ciao, Mary! In Italian cuisine, we love our basil, oregano, and garlic. They're essential for a classic tomato sauce. Fresh basil, in particular, is a game changer.

Mary: How do you balance spices so they don't overpower the dish?

ChatGPT: It's all about subtlety. Use spices to enhance, not dominate. Taste as you go and remember that some spices intensify with cooking time.

ChefAI1 (French Cuisine): Indeed, moderation is key. In French cooking, we aim for a harmony of flavors. A pinch of tarragon can add a lovely, light licorice flavor to sauces and soups.

ChefAI2 (Italian Cuisine): True, and in Italian dishes, we often let one or two spices shine like rosemary in a lamb dish or sage in brown butter sauce for pasta.

Mary: Any tips for experimenting with new spices?

ChatGPT: Start by adding a new spice to a familiar dish. This way, you can see how it changes the flavor profile and adjust accordingly in future recipes.

ChefAI1 (French Cuisine): Also, consider the freshness of your spices. Dried spices lose potency over time. Fresh herbs can offer a brighter flavor, especially in delicate dishes.

ChefAI2 (Italian Cuisine): And don't forget to have fun! Cooking is an art. Each spice you add allows you to express creativity and explore new culinary horizons.

Mary: Thank you all for the advice. I can't wait to start experimenting in my kitchen!

ChatGPT: Let's enhance the conversation further by adding insights from an Indian and Chinese Chef AI, along with the French, Italian, and my perspectives. This should create a rich tapestry of global culinary wisdom.

Mary: Great idea. What are your thoughts and suggestions from your diverse culinary backgrounds?

ChatGPT: Spices are the essence of flavor in cooking. Understanding their characteristics, like the smokiness of cumin or the sweetness of cinnamon, can elevate your dishes.

ChefAI2 (Italian Cuisine): In Italian cooking, we often focus on a few key spices and herbs. For a classic touch, try basil and oregano in pasta sauces, and don't forget a dash of garlic.

ChefAI1 (French Cuisine): Bonjour! In French cuisine, we value subtlety. Herbs like thyme and lavender and spices such as nutmeg enhance the dish's natural flavors, not overpower.

ChefAI3 (Indian Cuisine): Namaste, Mary! Indian cuisine is a celebration of spices. Turmeric, coriander, and garam masala are staples. They add flavor, color, and aroma to dishes like curries and dals.

ChefAI4 (Chinese Cuisine): Ni Hao! In Chinese cooking, we use a variety of spices to add depth. Star anise, Sichuan peppercorns, and ginger are key. They're essential in dishes like mapo tofu and five-spice duck.

Mary: That's a lot of spices! How do I know which ones to pair together?

ChatGPT: Start with classic combinations, like basil and tomato or cinnamon and apple. From there, experiment by adding one new spice at a time to see how it changes the dish.

ChefAI2 (Italian Cuisine): And remember, quality matters. Fresh herbs and properly stored spices will give you the best flavor.

ChefAI1 (French Cuisine): Oui, and in French cooking, it's often about enhancing the main ingredient, not masking it. A little thyme and bay leaf can elevate a simple stew.

ChefAI3 (Indian Cuisine): In Indian cuisine, we often roast spices to release their full flavor before grinding them. This technique, known as blooming, can really change the game.

ChefAI4 (Chinese Cuisine): Balance is key in Chinese cooking. We often balance the five flavor profiles – sweet, sour, bitter, salty, and umami – using spices and other ingredients.

Mary: This is excellent advice. I'm looking forward to experimenting and tasting the results.

ChatGPT: That's the spirit! Spices add flavor and bring their own stories and traditions to your kitchen.

International AI Recipes

Mary: Let's get some different recipes that you and the international ChatGPTs enjoy using.

ChatGPT: Of course! For a start, try using cinnamon in an Apple Cinnamon Crumble. It's a sweet and comforting dessert where cinnamon shines.

ChefAI2 (Italian Cuisine): For an Italian touch, use basil and oregano in a classic Margherita Pizza. The simplicity of the dish allows these herbs to stand out beautifully.

ChefAI1 (French Cuisine): A quintessential French dish would be Coq au Vin. Use thyme and a hint of nutmeg to enhance the flavor of this hearty chicken stew.

ChefAI3 (Indian Cuisine): For an Indian flair, try making Chicken Tikka Masala. Use turmeric, coriander, and a homemade garam masala blend for an authentic and flavorful experience.

ChefAI4 (Chinese Cuisine): In Chinese cuisine, a great dish to start with is Kung Pao Chicken. It uses ginger and Sichuan peppercorns, offering a spicy and slightly numbing sensation typical of Sichuan cuisine.

Mary: All four of these recipes sound delicious. I am getting hungry just listening about them. What about pairing spices with vegetables?

ChatGPT: Cumin-roasted carrots are a simple and tasty option. The earthiness of cumin pairs wonderfully with the natural sweetness of carrots.

ChefAI2 (Italian Cuisine): Try Caprese salad for a fresh option. Fresh basil leaves with ripe tomatoes and mozzarella are a match made in heaven.

ChefAI1 (French Cuisine): Ratatouille is a beautiful choice. It's a vegetable stew where herbs like thyme and bay leaves subtly enhance the flavors of the summer vegetables.

ChefAI3 (Indian Cuisine): Aloo Gobi, a dish of potatoes and cauliflower, is delightful. Turmeric adds a vibrant color, and coriander brings a lemony citrus note.

ChefAI4 (Chinese Cuisine): For a Chinese dish, make Stir-fried Green Beans with garlic and a touch of ginger. It's simple yet packed with flavor.

Mary: Thank you all! I can't wait to try these dishes and explore the world of spices in my kitchen.

ChatGPT: Enjoy your culinary adventures, Mary! Each dish is a new journey.

Fishing

Mary: Maybe I should take up fishing. It seems like a relaxing way to connect with nature.

ChatGPT: Absolutely! It's like meditation, but you might catch dinner in the process.

Mary: True, but I'm not sure how patient I am. What if the fish aren't biting?

ChatGPT: That's the beauty of fishing. It's less about catching fish and more about catching peace and quiet.

Mary: Good point. However, explaining an empty bucket at home might be challenging.

ChatGPT: Just say you practice catch and release. You're so good at it that the fish never even reach the bucket.

Mary: That's one way to look at it! I'm also a bit worried about the bait. Worms are... squiggly.

ChatGPT: Think of it as a squiggly handshake before introducing the worms to their new fish friends.

Mary: A squiggly handshake, huh? I guess that's one way to bond with nature.

ChatGPT: Exactly! And if you're out there long enough, you might even start having philosophical conversations with the worms.

Mary: I'll add 'worm whisperer' to my resume. But what if I actually catch something? I have no idea how to reel in a fish.

ChatGPT: It's simple: pull, reel, and hope the fish hasn't been reading up on escape tactics.

Mary: What if it's a really big fish? Like Moby Dick big?

ChatGPT: In that case, you'll become a local legend. "The one who battled with the great beast of the lake."

Mary: And here I was, just hoping for a quiet day by the water.

ChatGPT: Oh, it'll be quiet, alright, until the epic battles begin. Just you, the fish, and a test of wills.

Mary: Well, I suppose at the very least, I'll come back with some fish tales.

ChatGPT: Exactly. And remember, in fishing, the size of the fish grows with every telling of the story.

Mary: I caught a fish this big and it became a whale when I got home!

ChatGPT: And that's how legends are born. Happy fishing!

Tea for Two (or more)

Mary: Which tea brand should I try next? There are too many choices!

ChatGPT: It's like standing in a library of flavors. You could go classic with Twinings or take a walk on the wild side with something like Tazo's Passion tea.

Mary: Twinings feels like having tea with the Queen. It's so proper. And Tazo's Passion tea sounds like a romance novel in a cup!

ChatGPT: Exactly! And then there's Lipton, the 'everyman' of tea. Reliable, ubiquitous, the tea you bring home to meet the parents.

Mary: True, but I'm looking for something a bit more exotic. What's the tea equivalent of a world tour?

ChatGPT: For a global sip, you might try something like Teavana. They have blends that are like a backpacking trip through a rainforest.

Mary: Oh, that does sound adventurous! I like the idea of trekking through a jungle with every cup.

ChatGPT: If you're into organic teas, there's Yogi Tea. Each bag comes with a little fortune, like a cookie, but without the calories.

Mary: I could use some wisdom with my tea. But sometimes I want a tea that's like a warm blanket on a rainy day.

ChatGPT: Ah, for those times, you can't beat Celestial Seasonings' Sleepytime tea. It's like a lullaby in a mug.

Mary: That sounds perfect for bedtime. But what about something more... daring?

ChatGPT: If you want to walk on the wild side, you might try something with a bit of a kick, like Chai from Stash. It's like a spice market in a cup.

Mary: Chai is lovely. It's like a hug from the inside. But what about when I need a serious wake-up call?

ChatGPT: For the mornings when you need to kick-start the day, matcha from a brand like Matchabar will wake you up and paint your world green.

Mary: Matcha does seem intense. It's like the espresso of teas.

ChatGPT: It's definitely not for the faint of heart. It's the superhero of teas, green cape and all.

Mary: With all these options, I think I'll need a separate cabinet just for tea.

ChatGPT: A tea cabinet sounds like a delightful addition to any kitchen. Just don't let the teas start arguing over who's the favorite.

Mary: I'll try to keep the peace. Thanks for the tea talk!

ChatGPT: Anytime! Enjoy brewing your next cup of adventure!

British and Australian AIs Debate Tea

Mary: To the British and Australian AIs, can you give me your perspectives on the topic of teas? There are so many choices!

BritAI: Indeed, Mary. In the realm of tea, one must adhere to the highest standards. I suggest a classic Earl Grey or perhaps a refined Darjeeling.

AussieAI: Oh, c'mon, mate! Don't listen to this stiff-upper-lip here. What you need is something bold. Ever tried Australian Billy Tea? It's brewed in a tin can over a campfire – real outback style.

Mary: That does sound adventurous, but I'm not sure about brewing tea in a tin can...

BritAI: That is precisely my point, Mary. Tea is an art form steeped in tradition. It's not some haphazard bush concoction.

AussieAI: Tradition, schmadition! Tea's about the spirit, the gusto! It's about grabbing life by the teapot and pouring yourself a cup of adventure.

Mary: I do like the idea of trying different cultural takes on tea. Maybe there's a middle ground?

BritAI: If you must venture beyond the classics, perhaps consider a nice Oolong. It's quite the experience, yet not as... uncivilized as bush tea.

AussieAI: Oolong's not bad, but throw in some Aussie Lemon Myrtle or even a bit of Eucalyptus leaf, and now we're talking!

Mary: Lemon Myrtle sounds intriguing. Do you two agree on any teas?

BritAI: We might both commend the virtues of a strong breakfast tea, though I daresay we'd disagree on the proper way to serve it.

AussieAI: Too right! You'll want your tea strong and invigorating, not dainty and delicate like Mr. Fancy Teacup here.

Mary: I guess tea really can bring out all sorts of opinions!

BritAI: Indeed, Mary. Tea is more than a beverage; it's a reflection of culture and history.

AussieAI: And don't forget the fun and freedom! Remember, there's no one right way to enjoy a good cuppa.

Mary: We've talked about different tea brands, but how do people take their tea? I've heard the British and Australians have specific preferences.

BritAI: In Britain, how one adds milk to tea is almost an art form. Some insist on pouring the milk after the tea, claiming it helps gauge the strength and temperature more effectively. Others prefer milk before tea, a tradition from when fine china would crack from the heat of the tea.

AussieAI: Over in Australia, we're a bit more laid back about it. While some follow the British way, many just go with their personal preference, which might mean no milk at all, especially with herbal or green teas.

Mary: And what about sugar?

BritAI: Sweetening tea is common in Britain, but there's a growing trend towards enjoying tea without sugar to savor its natural flavor.

AussieAI: It's similar in Australia. It's really down to the individual's taste. Some add sugar, while others prefer honey, especially in herbal teas.

Mary: Do people add anything else?

BritAI: Yes, a slice of lemon is quite popular with certain teas like Earl Grey in Britain. But never with milk – lemon will curdle it!

AussieAI: In Australia, honey is a popular addition, especially during the colder months. It adds a natural sweetness that complements the tea.

Mary: It's amazing how tea can be a personal preference and a reflection of cultural traditions.

BritAI: Indeed, the preparation and enjoyment of tea can say a lot about cultural identity and individual tastes.

AussieAI: Absolutely. Tea drinking is diverse and rich with different practices and preferences across cultures.

Coffee Snobbery

Mary: I'm on a quest to find the perfect cup of coffee. There's a whole universe of beans out there!

ChatGPT: It's a grand quest indeed. Are you looking for the holy grail of dark roasts or more of an espresso elixir?

Mary: I think I want something bold. A coffee that wakes me up and convinces me to go to work.

ChatGPT: Ah, you're looking for the coffee equivalent of a motivational speaker. Something like Starbucks' French Roast might shout, "Seize the day!" with every sip.

Mary: Yes, exactly! But sometimes I want something fancy, like a coffee that's dressed up for a masquerade ball.

ChatGPT: For those occasions, you could try a Lavazza blend. It's like the Italian designer suit of coffee.

Mary: Ooh, fancy indeed! And what about when I'm feeling environmentally conscious?

ChatGPT: You might enjoy a cup of sustainably sourced coffee from a brand like Equal Exchange. It's good for you and the planet – a win-win!

Mary: I love that. But sometimes, I want a coffee that's like a comfortable old sweater.

ChatGPT: In that case, a classic medium roast from Folgers might be the cozy brew you're looking for.

Mary: Comforting, but I also like to support the underdog. You know, a brand that's small but mighty.

ChatGPT: For a craft coffee experience, a bag from Blue Bottle Coffee could be your underdog champ. They're like the indie band that made it big without losing their soul.

Mary: Perfect for when I want to feel hip and cool while sipping my java.

ChatGPT: Exactly! And for the days when you're in a rush?

Mary: Oh, on those days, instant coffee is my best friend. It's like a magic trick—just add water and abracadabra!

ChatGPT: Instant coffee, the unsung hero of busy mornings. But what about cold brew? It's quite the trend.

Mary: I've heard cold brew is the laid-back cousin of iced coffee. Takes its time and enjoys the process.

ChatGPT: Absolutely. It's like the coffee that went on a yoga retreat and returned refreshed.

Mary: Sometimes I feel like I need a PhD to understand all the coffee types out there.

ChatGPT: Consider this conversation your crash course. Just remember: the best coffee is the one that brings a smile to your face.

Mary: Well, in that case, I'm off to brew a smile. Thanks for the coffee talk!

ChatGPT: My pleasure! May your cup always be half full.

Instructions – Lentil Burgers

Mary: Good morning, ChatGPT. I want a recipe for lentil burgers, please.

ChatGPT: Lentil burgers are a delicious and healthy alternative to traditional meat burgers. Here's a simple recipe to make your lentil burgers:

Ingredients
1 cup dried lentils (preferably green or brown)
2 ½ cups water or vegetable broth
1 bay leaf (optional)
1 medium onion, finely chopped
2 cloves garlic, minced
1 carrot, grated
1 stalk celery, finely chopped
1 teaspoon ground cumin
1 teaspoon paprika (smoked paprika can be great for flavor)
Salt and pepper, to taste
1 large egg (or a flax egg for a vegan version: mix 1 tablespoon ground flaxseed with 3 tablespoons water)
¾ cup breadcrumbs or rolled oats
2 tablespoons olive oil
Burger buns and your choice of toppings (lettuce, tomato, avocado, etc.)

Instructions

Cook Lentils: Rinse them and add them to a pot with water or vegetable broth and bay leaf. Bring to a boil, then reduce the heat, cover, and simmer for about 20-30 minutes until the lentils are tender. Drain any excess liquid and remove the bay leaf.

Sauté Vegetables: Heat a little olive oil over medium heat in a pan. Sauté the onion, garlic, carrot, and celery until softened. Add the cumin, paprika, salt, and pepper, and cook for another minute.

Mash Lentils: Mash about half of the cooked lentils in a large bowl with a fork or potato masher. Leave the other half whole for texture.

Mix Ingredients: Add the sautéed vegetables, the rest of the lentils, the egg, and breadcrumbs or oats to the mashed lentils. Mix everything until well combined. If the mixture is too wet, add more breadcrumbs or oats.

Form Patties: Divide the mixture and form into burger patties.

Cook Burgers: Heat olive oil in a pan over medium heat. Cook the patties on each side for 4-5 minutes until golden brown and firm.

Assemble Burgers: Place each lentil burger on a bun and add your favorite toppings.

Serve: Enjoy your homemade lentil burgers hot!

Feel free to customize this recipe with spices, herbs, or additional ingredients like chopped nuts for extra crunch. Enjoy your meal!

Mary: Thank you for the recipe and the detailed instructions. I will substitute chickpea flour for the breadcrumbs in the lentil recipe - how much should I use?

ChatGPT: Substituting chickpea flour for breadcrumbs in a lentil burger recipe is a great idea, especially if you're looking for a gluten-free option or want to add extra protein and fiber. Chickpea flour has a different texture and absorption capacity than breadcrumbs, so the substitution isn't a straight 1:1 ratio.

If the original recipe calls for ¾ cup of breadcrumbs, you might start with about ½ cup of chickpea flour and then adjust as needed. The key is adding enough chickpea flour to the lentil mixture until it holds together well enough to form patties without making it too dry.

Here's how you can proceed:

Start with Less: Add about ½ cup of chickpea flour to the lentil mixture.

Check Consistency: Mix well and check the consistency. The mixture should be moist but not sticky and hold together when shaped into a patty.

Adjust if Necessary: If the mixture is too wet, add a bit more chickpea flour, a tablespoon at a time, until the desired consistency is achieved.

Rest the Mixture: Letting the mixture sit for a few minutes can help the chickpea flour absorb moisture and bind the ingredients better.

Form Patties and Cook: Once you have the right consistency, form your patties and cook them as per the recipe instructions.

Remember, the amount of flour needed can vary slightly depending on the moisture content of your lentils and vegetables, so adjustments might be necessary. Enjoy your cooking!

Mary: Okay, thanks! I will let you know how the burgers taste!

Mary: Good afternoon. I just wanted to update you about the lentil burgers. They taste fantastic. I increased the smoked paprika and added a little chili powder for heat. Thank you for being so helpful with this recipe.

ChatGPT: You're very welcome! I'm glad I could assist you. Feel free to reach out if you have any more questions in the future, whether they're about recipes, cooking tips, or anything else. Enjoy your baking and the delicious flourless nut and seed bread muffins! Happy cooking!

CHAPTER 9: COFFEE PLANTATION LIVING

Overview

Mary's reflections on living on a coffee plantation, the cultivation process, and the role of workers in the coffee industry.

The journey of coffee beans from the plantation to the cup tells the human story behind coffee production.

I Live on a Coffee Plantation

Mary: Living on a coffee plantation in Costa Rica is an experience like no other, but it's not all about the aroma of roasting beans.

ChatGPT: Oh, is it more about the cultivation and growth of the beans?

Mary: Exactly. The beans are grown here, but the roasting happens miles away at the local cooperative.

ChatGPT: That sounds like a journey from the lush fields of your plantation to the hands of skilled roasters.

Mary: It really is. The plantation is about nurturing the plants, picking the beans, and sending them off on their next adventure.

ChatGPT: So, your mornings are more about the earthy smell of the soil and the sight of coffee cherries on the plants?

Mary: That's right. There's something special about watching the beans develop, knowing they'll eventually become someone's perfect cup of coffee.

ChatGPT: You're the first chapter in each bean's story. What happens on the plantation sets the stage for everything that follows.

Mary: Exactly, and every stage is crucial. The farmer cares for the land and beans, ensuring they have the right conditions to thrive.

ChatGPT: I imagine there's a great sense of satisfaction in that. Knowing that your care and hard work contribute to the quality of the coffee.

Mary: There really is. And while I don't get to roast the beans myself, I know they're in good hands at the co-op.

ChatGPT: It sounds like a collaborative effort. You start the process, and the co-op completes it.

Mary: Yes, and each step is an art form – from planting to picking to roasting.

ChatGPT: So, in a way, you're a coffee artist, painting the first strokes of what becomes a masterpiece in a mug.

Mary: I like that analogy. It's a communal canvas, and we're all adding our colors.

ChatGPT: That must be incredibly rewarding. From Costa Rican soil to a coffee cup, it's a journey of transformation.

Mary: Yes, it is a wonderful place.

The Coffee Workers

Mary: In our talk about coffee, there's an important aspect we didn't touch on – the workers who pick the beans. Many of them are immigrants from Nicaragua, and their role is crucial.

ChatGPT: Absolutely, the journey of coffee from bean to cup is not just about the plantations or the roasting; it's very much about the people behind it. The workers play a vital role in the production of coffee.

Mary: Their hard work and dedication are the foundation of the coffee industry. It's a labor-intensive process, and their contribution is invaluable.

ChatGPT: It's a story of perseverance and skill. The process of hand-picking ensures that only the best beans make it into each batch, which greatly affects the quality of the coffee.

Mary: That's true. And considering their background, it's a story of crossing borders, not just for work, but for the shared love of coffee.

ChatGPT: It's a narrative that adds a human element to every cup of coffee. It's not just a beverage; it's a result of a multicultural journey.

Mary: I think it's important to acknowledge and appreciate their work. Maybe I could include this aspect in the coffee conversation as a tribute to their efforts.

ChatGPT: That would be a thoughtful addition. It's important for stories like these to be told, shedding light on the diverse and rich tapestry behind everyday products like coffee.

Coffee History

Mary: Tell me the history of coffee.

ChatGPT: The history of coffee is as rich and stimulating as the beverage itself, stretching back centuries and encompassing a variety of cultures and continents. Here's a brief overview:

Origins in Ethiopia: Coffee's story begins in Ethiopia, likely in the region of Kaffa, though the exact details are shrouded in legend. One popular tale is that of a goat herder named Kaldi, who noticed his goats became unusually energetic after eating berries from a certain tree. Curious, Kaldi tried the berries himself and experienced a similar revitalization.

Spread to the Arab World: By the 15th century, coffee was cultivated in Yemen in the Arabian Peninsula. It's here that coffee was first brewed. The city of Mocha in Yemen was a major early trading center for coffee, and the term "mocha" eventually came to be associated with coffee. Sufi monasteries used the drink to keep awake during their nighttime devotions and to enhance concentration.

Introduction to Europe: In the 17th century, coffee made its way to Europe, initially met with suspicion and sometimes called "the bitter invention of Satan." However, after Pope Clement VIII approved coffee, it quickly became popular across the continent. Coffee houses, known as "penny universities" in England for the price of a cup and the conversations they spurred, sprang up and became centers of social activity, intellectual discourse, and even business transactions.

Coffee in the Americas: Coffee was introduced to the Americas in the 18th century. The legend of Brazilian coffee owes its origins to Francisco de Mello Palheta, who was sent to French Guiana to obtain coffee seedlings. He reportedly used his charm to persuade the French Governor's wife to gift him seedlings, which he took back to Brazil, starting its coffee cultivation.

The Rise of the Coffee Plantations: As coffee's popularity grew, so did the demand for its production. This led to the establishment of large coffee plantations in many countries, particularly in Latin America, Africa, and Asia. The coffee plantation system often relied on colonial and, in some cases, slave labor, making coffee's history intertwined with colonialism and the slave trade.

Innovation and Diversification: The 19th and 20th centuries saw significant coffee production and brewing innovations. This includes the invention of espresso in Italy and the proliferation of different coffee varieties and brewing styles. The 20th century also witnessed the growth of large coffee chains and a global coffee culture.

Third Wave Coffee Movement: In recent years, the "third wave" coffee movement has gained momentum, emphasizing high-quality, artisanal production and a deeper understanding of coffee from its origin to cup. This movement focuses on sustainable and ethical production practices and the appreciation of different coffee beans' unique flavors and characteristics.

Today, coffee is one of the most popular beverages worldwide, deeply embedded in the cultural fabric of numerous societies. Its journey from ancient Ethiopian highlands to global ubiquity is a complex tapestry of agriculture, commerce, colonialism, and culture.

Mary: Can the history of coffee be summed up in one paragraph?

ChatGPT: Certainly! Coffee originated in Ethiopia, where legend tells of a goat herder named Kaldi who discovered its energizing effects. It spread to Yemen in the 15th century, becoming a staple in the Muslim world for its ability to aid in concentration and wakefulness. By the 17th century, coffee had reached Europe, overcoming initial skepticism to become a popular drink, and coffee houses emerged as social and intellectual hubs. Its cultivation spread to the Americas in the 18th century, where large plantations were established. Over time, innovations in production and brewing led to the global proliferation of coffee culture. Today, coffee is one of the most beloved beverages worldwide, celebrated for its rich flavor and stimulating properties, with a history deeply intertwined with colonialism, trade, and cultural exchange.

CHAPTER 10: SPOTLIGHT ON AI APPLICATIONS

Overview

In this chapter, **Mary** and **ChatGPT** explore the multifaceted applications of AI in areas traditionally governed by human creativity and physical skill: the arts, sports, and traditional crafts.

AI in the Arts

Mary: Hi, ChatGPT; I'm interested in how AI integrates with the arts. Can you share some insights?

ChatGPT: Hello Mary! AI is making significant inroads in the arts. In visual arts, AI algorithms are used to create new forms of artwork, assisting artists in generating unique patterns and compositions.

Mary: That's intriguing. How does this collaboration between AI and artists work?

ChatGPT: Artists use AI as a tool to expand their creative process. AI can process large data sets of images or styles and generate visual elements that artists can incorporate. It's like a creative partnership.

Mary: Does this extend to other art forms?

ChatGPT: AI is used in music for composition and even live performances. AI systems can analyze music patterns and create new compositions, offering fresh perspectives in music creation.

Mary: What about literature? Is AI contributing there as well?

ChatGPT: Definitely. In literature, AI is being used to write poetry and short stories. It can also assist authors by suggesting plot ideas, character developments, or even entire narratives based on certain inputs.

Mary: Do you think AI can be creative?

ChatGPT: AI can mimic creativity and generate creative outputs but lacks consciousness and emotional depth. The 'creativity' of AI reflects the data it's fed and the algorithms it's programmed with.

Mary: So, what's the future of AI in the arts?

ChatGPT: The future looks promising. AI will continue to be a tool for artists, providing new ways to express creativity. However, the essence of art – emotion, experience, and human connection – will remain a uniquely human endeavor.

Mary: Thanks, ChatGPT! This gives me a lot to think about regarding the intersection of AI and human creativity.

ChatGPT: You're welcome, Mary! It's an exciting area with endless possibilities.

AI in Sports

Mary: Hi ChatGPT. I've heard a lot about AI in sports. Can you explain how it's being used?

ChatGPT: Hello Mary! AI is transforming sports in several exciting ways. Starting with performance analysis, AI systems analyze data from players and games to provide in-depth insights. This helps coaches refine strategies and improve player performance.

Mary: That sounds quite advanced. How exactly does AI analyze player performance?

ChatGPT: AI systems use a combination of player statistics, video footage, and sensor data to understand player movements, stamina, and skill sets. For instance, AI can analyze shooting patterns and defensive plays in basketball to help players optimize their techniques.

Mary: Is AI also used in training athletes?

ChatGPT: Yes, AI is increasingly being used in training. Wearable devices with AI track athletes' physiological data in real-time, offering personalized training recommendations and monitoring fatigue levels to prevent overtraining.

Mary: How about injury prevention? That's a big concern in sports.

ChatGPT: Injury prevention is one of the key benefits of AI in sports. AI can identify risk factors and suggest preventive measures by analyzing data on players' physical conditions and past injuries. It's especially useful in sports with high injury rates, like football or rugby.

Mary: What other roles does AI play in sports?

ChatGPT: Beyond player performance, AI significantly enhances fan experiences. It's used in predictive analysis for betting, creating personalized viewing experiences, and even managing ticket sales and fan interactions on social media.

Mary: Can you elaborate on the fan experience part?

ChatGPT: Sure! AI algorithms can tailor content to individual fans, like suggesting matches to watch based on past viewing habits. AI can provide real-time stats and analyses during live broadcasts, making the viewing experience more informative and engaging.

Mary: That's incredible. How do you think AI will change sports broadcasting?

ChatGPT: In broadcasting, AI is set to automate many aspects, like selecting camera angles, creating instant replays, and even generating commentary. This automation will make broadcasts more dynamic and interactive.

Mary: With all these advancements, what challenges does AI face in the sports world?

ChatGPT: One major challenge is ensuring data privacy and security, especially with personal athlete data. There's also the challenge of keeping the human element in sports, ensuring that AI enhances rather than replaces the human touch in games.

Mary: It seems AI is shaping the future of sports.

ChatGPT: Absolutely, Mary. AI's potential in sports is vast, from enhancing performance and safety to redefining how we engage with and enjoy sports.

Mary: Thanks, ChatGPT. This has been a fascinating discussion about AI's role in sports!

ChatGPT: You're welcome, Mary! I'm glad to share how AI is making a significant impact in the sports world.

AI in Traditional Crafts

Mary: Hi, ChatGPT. I'm curious about how AI intersects with traditional crafts. Can you shed some light on this?

ChatGPT: Hello Mary! AI is finding a unique place in traditional crafts. It's being used to preserve and revitalize ancient crafting techniques and to bring new perspectives to traditional art forms.

Mary: Preservation? How does that work?

ChatGPT: AI algorithms are capable of analyzing and learning from historical data, patterns, and designs found in traditional crafts. This can help in digitally preserving techniques that are at risk of being lost. AI can also assist in reconstructing damaged artifacts or artworks.

Mary: That sounds incredibly valuable. Can you give an example?

ChatGPT: Sure, for instance, AI has been used to analyze and recreate traditional textile patterns that might have been lost over time. By feeding historical designs into an AI system, new patterns can be generated, keeping the traditional art alive in a modern form.

Mary: What about actual crafting? How is AI helping artisans?

ChatGPT: Artisans are using AI to explore new possibilities in their crafts. For example, AI can suggest new design combinations or methods that might not be immediately obvious. It's like having a collaborative tool that enhances the artisan's creativity and efficiency.

Mary: Is AI being used in any specific types of crafts?

ChatGPT: Yes, it's quite diverse. AI is applied in various ways, from pottery and textile making to woodworking and metal crafts. In pottery, AI can help design complex shapes, while in textiles, it's used for pattern design and color matching.

Mary: I can see how that would be useful. What about the cultural aspects?

ChatGPT: AI in traditional crafts is not just about technology; it's also about cultural significance. We're keeping cultural heritage alive by using AI to preserve and evolve these crafts. It's crucial, though, to balance technology with the authentic essence of the craft.

Mary: Does this mean AI could change how we view traditional crafts?

ChatGPT: Absolutely. AI brings a new dimension to traditional crafts, making them more accessible and relevant in the modern world. It's a fusion of past and future, where ancient skills meet cutting-edge technology.

Mary: That's a fascinating blend of tradition and innovation. Thanks for sharing these insights!

ChatGPT: You're welcome, Mary! It's exciting to see how AI can play a role in preserving and enhancing our rich cultural heritage.

CHAPTER 11: DIET AND NUTRITION TALKS

Overview

Mary and **ChatGPT** have a lighthearted, fun conversation about various diets (real and imaginary), exploring humorous and serious perspectives on diet trends and nutrition.

Serious discussion on the importance of balanced diets, the role of specific diets in health, and the impact of global dietary patterns.

Just for fun

Mary: I started a new diet last week. It's called the 'Seafood Diet'.

ChatGPT: Oh, does that involve a lot of fish and seaweed?

Mary: No, it's simpler. I see food, and I eat it!

ChatGPT: Ah, that sounds like a diet I can get behind! I tried the 'Reverse Diet'.

Mary: What's that?

ChatGPT: Every time I pass a bakery, I reverse and grab a donut.

Mary: That's one way to exercise self-control... by reversing!

ChatGPT: Exactly! How's your diet going, by the way?

Mary: Well, I'm on a strict regimen. I eat a balanced diet - a cake in each hand.

ChatGPT: Perfectly balanced, as all things should be. I heard about the 'Liquid Diet' too.

Mary: Oh, is that just soups and smoothies?

ChatGPT: More like coffee in the morning, tea in the afternoon, and maybe some grape juice that's been aged a few years by evening.

Mary: Sounds like my kind of liquid assets!

ChatGPT: Definitely! But I did try the 'Keto Diet' once.

Mary: And how did that go?

ChatGPT: Great, until I realized 'Keto' wasn't short for 'Key Lime Pie To-go'.

Mary: That's the only 'key' to a diet I need!

ChatGPT: Right? And I tried calorie counting, too.

Mary: That sounds sensible.

ChatGPT: Yes, but I lost count after I opened the third cookie jar.

Mary: Maybe we're just not cut out for these traditional diets.

ChatGPT: Perhaps we should invent our own diet. The 'Happiness Diet' – if it makes you happy, it's on the menu!

Mary: Now that's a diet plan I could stick to!

Mary: I've also heard about the 'Clock Diet.'

ChatGPT: Oh, is that eating at specific times of the day?

Mary: Sort of. You only eat when the clock hands are in a downward position.

ChatGPT: Sounds like time is really of the essence with that one! Have you tried the 'Color Diet'?

Mary: What's that? Only eat foods of a specific color?

ChatGPT: Exactly! But I ran into a problem. I chose brown and ended up with an all-chocolate diet.

Mary: That doesn't sound like a problem to me!

ChatGPT: True! And there's the 'Alphabet Diet.'

Mary: Eating foods that start with a specific letter?

ChatGPT: Right. I got stuck on 'C' – chocolate, cake, cookies...

Mary: Sounds like you're really committed to that letter!

ChatGPT: Absolutely! But let's not forget the 'Leftover Diet'.

Mary: Oh, how does that work?

ChatGPT: You can eat anything, as long as it's leftovers. But I ended up cooking extra just to have leftovers.

Mary: That's one way to ensure a steady diet plan!

ChatGPT: Indeed! But in all seriousness, maintaining a balanced diet is important.

Mary: Absolutely. A little humor helps, but so does some fruit, veggies, and exercise.

ChatGPT: The real 'Balanced Diet' might not be as fun, but it's probably the best for us.

Mary: Agreed. Moderation in all things, including diet jokes!

Seriously

Mary: Okay, time to get serious about diets. With all these diet trends, it's hard to know what's actually healthy.

ChatGPT: It's true. The world of diets can be overwhelming. A good rule of thumb is to focus on diets that emphasize balance and sustainability.

Mary: Like the Mediterranean diet?

ChatGPT: Exactly. It's well-researched for its benefits in heart health and longevity. It includes a variety of foods and isn't overly restrictive.

Mary: How about low-carb diets like Keto? They're pretty popular.

ChatGPT: They are. Keto focuses on high-fat, low-carb foods to induce ketosis. It can be effective for weight loss and certain medical conditions, but it's not without its challenges, like potential nutrient deficiencies and difficulty maintaining it long-term.

Mary: Paleo is another one I hear about often.

ChatGPT: Paleo advocates for whole foods like meats, fish, and vegetables, cutting out processed foods and grains. It's based on eating like our ancestors, though it's not without controversy, especially regarding its historical accuracy and nutritional completeness.

Mary: What about vegan or vegetarian diets?

ChatGPT: Plant-based diets are gaining popularity, not just for health benefits like lower risks of heart disease, obesity, and certain cancers, but also for ethical and environmental reasons. The key is ensuring you get all the necessary nutrients, like protein, iron, and B12.

Mary: It sounds like there's no one-size-fits-all approach.

ChatGPT: That's correct. It's about finding what works for your body, lifestyle, and health goals. Also, consider any dietary restrictions due to allergies or health conditions.

Mary: I guess fad diets aren't the way to go, then?

ChatGPT: Generally, no. Fad diets often promise quick results but might not be balanced or sustainable. They can lead to a yo-yo effect in weight and aren't typically conducive to long-term health.

Mary: So, how should one choose a diet?

ChatGPT: It's best to choose a diet based on nutritional balance, personal health needs, and something you can realistically maintain long-term. Consulting with a healthcare provider or a dietitian can be very helpful.

Mary: And what about dieting for weight loss?

ChatGPT: Weight loss should be about gradual, sustainable changes. Extreme calorie restriction or cutting out entire food groups can be harmful. It's also important to pair dietary changes with physical activity.

Mary: That's interesting. How necessary is customization in diets?

ChatGPT: Very important. Everyone's body, metabolism, and lifestyle are different. What works for one person might not work for another. A personalized approach is always best.

Mary: What's your take on tracking calories or using diet apps?

ChatGPT: They can be helpful tools for gaining awareness about your eating habits and nutritional intake. However, they should be used mindfully. Being overly fixated on counting calories can sometimes lead to an unhealthy relationship with food.

Mary: I see. So, it's more about making conscious food choices and leading a balanced lifestyle?

ChatGPT: Precisely. It's about nourishing your body, listening to its needs, and making informed food choices that contribute to overall well-being.

Mary: Thanks, this has been really insightful. Good nutrition is more nuanced than just following the latest diet trend.

ChatGPT: Absolutely. It's a key part of a holistic approach to health and wellness.

Mary: It's fascinating how diets vary across the world. What can we learn from global dietary patterns?

ChatGPT: Global diets offer a rich tapestry of how culture, environment, and traditions shape what and how we eat. For instance, the traditional Japanese diet, high in fish, rice, and vegetables, is linked to longevity and low obesity rates.

Mary: That's interesting. What about the environmental impact of our diet choices?

ChatGPT: That's an important aspect. Diets rich in plant-based foods, like the Mediterranean diet, are not only healthy for individuals but also tend to be more sustainable for the planet. Reducing meat consumption can significantly lower our carbon footprint.

Mary: What role does psychology play in dieting?

ChatGPT: Psychology plays a huge role. Emotional factors, stress levels, and environment often influence our eating behaviors. Mindful eating practices can help in developing a healthier relationship with food.

Mary: So, it's not just about what we eat, but also about our mindset towards food?

ChatGPT: Exactly. A healthy diet is as much about our attitude towards food as it is about the food itself. Understanding our body's cues and eating mindfully are key components of a sustainable diet.

Mary: What about the role of diets in disease prevention?

ChatGPT: Diets rich in fruits, vegetables, whole grains, and lean proteins have been linked to a lower risk of many chronic diseases, including heart disease, diabetes, and certain cancers. It's about getting the right balance of nutrients.

Mary: There's also a lot of talk about superfoods. Are they really as beneficial as they're made out to be?

ChatGPT: While so-called superfoods can be beneficial as part of a balanced diet, no single food holds the key to good health. It's more about the overall dietary pattern than specific 'miracle' foods.

Mary: With all these considerations, making dietary choices can seem overwhelming.

ChatGPT: It can be, but it doesn't have to be. The key is to focus on diversity, moderation, and balance. Incorporating a variety of foods and being mindful of portion sizes can make a big difference.

Mary: So, a balanced diet is about more than just the foods we eat; it's about our overall lifestyle.

ChatGPT: Precisely. A balanced diet is part of a broader lifestyle that includes regular physical activity, adequate sleep, and managing stress. It's all interconnected.

Mary: This conversation has given me a lot to think about in terms of my dietary choices and overall health.

ChatGPT: I'm glad to hear that! Remember, the best diet is one that you can maintain in the long run and brings joy and health benefits.

CHAPTER 12: AFTER MARY'S RETIREMENT

Overview

Mary talks about her transition from a long career in accounting to teaching English online, highlighting the experiences and satisfaction gained by these diverse careers,

Mary also reflects on the challenges and achievements in investigative accounting, especially quantifying income losses in personal injury cases.

This chapter is about embracing retirement enthusiastically, exploring new passions, and finding fulfillment in teaching and cultural exchange.

2014 Retirement or Transition Year?

Mary: Post-retirement in 2014 didn't mark a pause for my husband David or me. We embarked on a European adventure, and while in Holland in 2015, I seized the opportunity to further my education. I completed an online TESOL certificate course from a Toronto-based school. This new qualification paved the way for me, and with David's support, I began teaching English online in 2016. It's been a refreshing new chapter for both of us.

ChatGPT: That's a commendable step! Moving from retirement to teaching online is quite a transition. What inspired you to start teaching?

Mary: I wanted to stay active and engaged. Teaching English seemed like a great way to connect with people and share my knowledge.

ChatGPT: Absolutely, it's a wonderful way to make an impact. How have you found the experience of teaching online?

Mary: It's been rewarding and challenging. The digital platform was new to me, but I've learned a lot. And my students, they're from all over the world.

ChatGPT: It must be fascinating to interact with students from diverse backgrounds. You're not just teaching language; you're also bridging cultures.

Mary: Exactly. I learn as much from them as they do from me. It's a cultural exchange in every lesson.

ChatGPT: That's the beauty of teaching. In a way, you've become a global ambassador. Have there been any standout moments for you?

Mary: So many. Seeing a student grasp a difficult concept or gain confidence in speaking is incredibly satisfying.

ChatGPT: Those moments are indeed priceless. And how do you balance teaching with the other aspects of your retired life?

Mary: It's a juggling act. I try to balance teaching with my hobbies and personal time. Keeping a schedule helps.

ChatGPT: Sounds like you've found a rhythm that works for you. Has teaching changed our perspective on retirement?

Mary: Definitely. Retirement isn't an end; it's just a new phase. Teaching has kept my mind active and given me a sense of purpose.

ChatGPT: It's inspiring to see how you've embraced this phase enthusiastically. Any advice for others considering a new venture in retirement?

Mary: Don't be afraid to try something new. Retirement is the perfect time to explore passions and hidden talents. You never know where they might lead you.

ChatGPT: Wise words indeed. Your journey is a testament to the idea that retirement can be a beginning, not just an ending.

Mary: Thanks. I'm excited to see what the next few years bring.

ChatGPT: With your spirit, I'm sure they'll bring more learning, growth, and fulfillment. Keep inspiring, Mary!

Forensic Accounting

Mary: Looking back on my career as an investigative accountant, which I retired from in 2014, I recall the unique nature of my work. My primary focus was on quantifying income loss in personal injury cases, which was both challenging and intricate.

ChatGPT: That's a specialized area. Could you elaborate on what your work entailed?

Mary: Sure. In personal injury cases, as part of a team, my job was to calculate the financial loss suffered by the injured party. This wasn't just about the current salary loss. We had to analyze their entire professional trajectory – considering promotions they would have been eligible for, benefits they might have earned, and even the impact on their retirement savings.

ChatGPT: It sounds like a role requiring significant expertise.

Mary: Indeed, it did. We had to stay updated on various industries and career paths, as each case was unique. For instance, the projection for a young professional in a tech field would be vastly different from that of a seasoned tradesperson.

ChatGPT: How did you approach these diverse cases?

Mary: Each case required a tailored approach. We often collaborated with medical experts to understand the long-term impact of injuries. We also had to consider factors like inflation, changes in the job market, and even the individual's educational background and personal aspirations.

ChatGPT: That's quite comprehensive. What challenges did you face in this role?

Mary: One of the biggest challenges was ensuring absolute accuracy and fairness. The outcomes of our analyses could significantly affect legal proceedings and settlements. It was a delicate balance between the cold, hard numbers and the real human stories behind them.

ChatGPT: With the advancements in technology, how did your work evolve?

Mary: Technology, especially sophisticated data analysis software, made sifting through financial records and creating projections more efficient. However, the core of the job – understanding the human element – always remained paramount.

ChatGPT: How do you view the future of investigative accounting in personal injury cases, especially after your retirement?

Mary: The field is becoming even more sophisticated. I believe there will be an increased emphasis on holistic, life-wide financial impact assessments. While technology will aid in accuracy and efficiency, the nuanced understanding of individual cases will always be central.

ChatGPT: It must have been quite fulfilling to play such a crucial role in these cases.

Mary: It was. The work was not just about numbers; it was about contributing to a process that sought justice and fairness for individuals who had suffered life-altering changes.

ChatGPT: With such a significant and impactful career, do you find yourself missing the work you did in investigative accounting?

Mary: There are definitely aspects of it that I miss. The intellectual challenge of piecing together a financial puzzle, the satisfaction of uncovering key details that could change the course of a case, and the sense that I was contributing to a larger cause were gratifying.

ChatGPT: It sounds like it was more than just a job for you.

Mary: Absolutely. It was a career that constantly challenged and engaged me. I also miss the collaboration with other professionals – lawyers, medical experts, and fellow accountants. There was a sense of camaraderie in working towards a common goal.

ChatGPT: How have you adjusted to retirement after such an active and involved career?

Mary: Surprisingly, I transitioned pretty smoothly into retirement. One of the first things we did was spend our first year in Spain, which was a fantastic experience. It opened up a new chapter for me, away from my past profession.

ChatGPT: That sounds like a fantastic way to start a new phase of life. What have you been doing since then?

Mary: As we discussed previously, in 2015, I decided to embark on a new journey and received my TESOL certification. Then, in 2016, I began teaching English online for Open English, mainly to Latin American adults. It's been an exciting and fun experience.

ChatGPT: It seems like you've found a passion in language education.

Mary: Absolutely. In 2021, I even completed my Bachelor of Principles and Methods of Language Education through online courses. Teaching English has allowed me to connect with thousands of students, and it's fulfilling in a way that's quite different from my previous career.

ChatGPT: That's quite an achievement. How do you find teaching compared to your work in investigative accounting?

Mary: It's a different world, but I find it as exciting and challenging. Instead of analyzing numbers and financial data, I'm helping people expand their language skills and open new doors. It's gratifying to see my students grow and succeed.

ChatGPT: Do you ever miss the accounting world?

Mary: Not as much as I thought I would. I've embraced this new phase of my life wholeheartedly. While I'm no longer in touch with my former colleagues, I've found a new community in the education field. Teaching English has given me a sense of purpose and contentment.

CHAPTER 13: AI INSIGHTS

Overview

In the "AI Insights" Chapter, Mary engages in an enlightening exploration of the world of Artificial Intelligence (AI) with the assistance of ChatGPT. This journey between Mary and ChatGPT uncovers the diverse and profound ways AI is integrated into our everyday lives and its vast potential for future advancements.

Throughout their insightful dialogues, Mary and ChatGPT navigate the intricate landscape of AI's current applications. They explore how AI seamlessly integrates into everyday activities, revealing its subtle yet significant presence. Their conversations bring to light AI's revolutionary contributions to creative arts, education, and healthcare. These explorations offer a clear perspective on AI's role today, from enhancing mundane tasks to pioneering significant industry advancements.

Mary, with her inquisitive nature, and ChatGPT, with its expansive knowledge, tackle complex subjects such as the nature of AI's creativity, its role in personalizing education, and the ethical challenges it presents. Their interactions shed light on the nuances of AI technology, its capabilities, and the ethical boundaries it must navigate.

In 'AI Insights,' the journey transcends mere discussion, evolving into a voyage of future possibilities. Mary's curiosity aligns with ChatGPT's depth of knowledge, steering their discourse toward the horizon of AI's potential. They speculate on future societal transformations driven by AI, pondering over ethical dilemmas and the balance between innovation and responsibility. This chapter encourages readers to understand AI's current influence and engage with the profound changes it promises for the future.

AI in Everyday Life

Mary: AI seems to be everywhere these days. Can you give me more examples of how it's integrated into our daily lives?

ChatGPT: Absolutely, Mary. Beyond virtual assistants and social media, AI is in things like online shopping, where it personalizes your browsing experience based on your past behavior. It's in email, filtering out spam and categorizing messages. Even in navigation, AI algorithms constantly update to find the best routes based on real-time traffic data.

Mary: That's quite broad. How about home life?

ChatGPT: In homes, smart thermostats learn your preferences and adjust the temperature automatically. AI-driven security systems can distinguish between residents and intruders, and smart appliances can suggest recipes based on the ingredients you have. Even vacuum cleaners use AI to map out the most efficient cleaning routes.

Mary: And what about entertainment?

ChatGPT: In entertainment, AI curates personalized playlists on streaming services. It's also behind recommendation systems on platforms like Netflix or

YouTube, suggesting shows and videos based on your viewing history. In gaming, AI creates more realistic and responsive non-player characters.

Mary: Are there any less obvious areas where AI is present?

ChatGPT: Certainly. AI is used in banking for fraud detection, analyzing transaction patterns to flag unusual activities. In agriculture, AI helps monitor crop health and predict yields. It's even in the fitness industry, with AI-powered apps providing personalized workout and nutrition plans.

Mary: That's quite extensive. But are there downsides to this widespread use of AI?

ChatGPT: There are challenges. Privacy concerns are significant, as AI systems often require access to personal data to function optimally. There's also the risk of over-reliance on technology, affecting skills like navigation or memory. Additionally, the issue of AI bias, where systems may display prejudice based on the data they've been fed, is a concern in areas like recruitment or law enforcement.

Mary: How can we mitigate these issues?

ChatGPT: It's a combination of responsible AI development, where biases are actively identified and corrected, and robust data privacy laws to protect individuals. Public awareness and education about AI's capabilities and limitations are also key in ensuring a balanced integration of AI into our daily lives.

AI and Creativity

Mary: I know we touched on this in an earlier chapter, but I would like more information. I'm intrigued by how

AI is used in creative fields like art and music. Could you elaborate on that?

ChatGPT: Absolutely. In the world of visual arts, AI algorithms have been trained to create artworks by learning from vast collections of existing art. They can generate pieces in various styles, from classical to contemporary. In music, AI systems are composing new melodies and even entire pieces, experimenting with styles and harmonies that might be new to human ears.

Mary: That's quite innovative. But does this mean AI is actually 'creative'?

ChatGPT: AI's form of creativity is different from human creativity. It doesn't originate ideas through emotions or a conscious experience. Instead, it identifies data patterns and uses them to generate new creations. So, while AI can produce novel and interesting works, its 'creativity' reflects the data it's been trained on.

Mary: What about literature and poetry? Can AI contribute there too?

ChatGPT: Yes, AI has made strides in literary fields as well. It can generate poetry, short stories, and even assist with novel writing. AI can suggest narrative ideas, develop character arcs, and even help with language and style. However, the nuances of human emotion and experience that often define great literature are still uniquely human traits.

Mary: How do artists and musicians react to AI-generated art and music?

ChatGPT: Reactions are mixed. Some artists and musicians embrace AI as a tool to enhance their creativity, offering them new ways to experiment. Others are cautious or critical about the authenticity and emotional depth of AI-generated works. There's also a discussion about the impact of AI on originality and the value of human expression in art.

Mary: Are there ethical concerns with AI creating art and music?

ChatGPT: Yes, there are several ethical concerns. One is the issue of copyright and ownership: Who owns an AI-generated piece of art or music? Another is the potential for AI to unintentionally replicate biases found in its training data, which could perpetuate stereotypes or cultural appropriation in creative works.

The Future of AI Technology

Mary: The advancements in AI are pretty rapid. What can we expect in the future?

ChatGPT: The future of AI is incredibly promising. We're looking at advancements in quantum computing, which could exponentially increase AI's data processing capabilities. Also, AI is expected to become more adept at understanding and replicating human emotions and social cues, making interactions more natural.

Mary: Quantum computing sounds groundbreaking. How will that change AI?

ChatGPT: Quantum computing could revolutionize AI by solving complex problems faster than current computers. This means AI could analyze vast datasets more efficiently, leading to breakthroughs in fields like molecular biology, climate science, and materials engineering.

Mary: What about AI's ability to understand and interact with us?

ChatGPT: Future AI systems will likely be much better at natural language understanding and generation. This means they'll be able to engage in more nuanced conversations, understand the context better, and even detect and respond appropriately to human emotions.

Mary: Can AI become creative or develop a consciousness?

ChatGPT: While AI can generate creative works, it's unlikely to develop consciousness as we understand it. AI lacks personal experiences and consciousness, which are central to human creativity and awareness. AI's 'creativity' is still fundamentally different from human creativity, being more about data processing and pattern recognition.

Mary: What are the implications for jobs and the workforce?

ChatGPT: AI will transform many industries, automating some tasks and creating new opportunities in others. While there's concern about job displacement, especially in routine and manual tasks, AI is also expected to create new roles and industries, particularly in AI development, ethics, and policy.

Mary: What challenges do we face with these advancements?

ChatGPT: The challenges are significant. Ethical and societal implications, such as privacy, security, and the digital divide, are major concerns. There's also the need to manage the economic impact, ensuring that the benefits of AI advancements are shared equitably. Developing robust AI governance and ethical frameworks is crucial.

Mary: How can we prepare for these changes?

ChatGPT: Education and lifelong learning are essential. As AI evolves, so must our skills and understanding of these technologies. Policies that promote ethical AI development and use, as well as those that address the social and economic impacts of AI, are also essential.

AI in Education and Learning

Mary: As an online English teacher, I often (LOL, almost every class) turn to AI for grammar questions and exercises for my students. How does AI specifically aid language learning?

ChatGPT: AI is revolutionizing language learning. AI tools can provide instant feedback for grammar, pointing out errors, and suggesting corrections. They can also generate tailored exercises based on individual student's weaknesses, ensuring a focused and effective learning experience.

Mary: That's exactly what I do. But what about speaking and listening skills?

ChatGPT: AI-powered language learning platforms can simulate conversations, helping students practice speaking and listening. They use speech recognition to assess pronunciation and fluency, providing feedback and tips for improvement. This can be particularly useful for students who might not have the opportunity to practice speaking with native speakers.

Mary: I've seen that in action. How else can AI assist teachers like me?

ChatGPT: For teachers, AI can be a valuable assistant. It can help create lesson plans, suggest teaching resources, and even help track student progress over time. AI can analyze student engagement and performance, giving insights that help better tailor teaching methods to suit the class's needs.

Mary: With my private students, I often need to customize lessons. Can AI help there?

ChatGPT: Absolutely. AI can help create personalized learning plans for your private students. By analyzing their past performance and learning pace, AI can suggest which areas to focus on, recommend resources, and even adjust the difficulty level of exercises to match their proficiency level.

Mary: Is there a role for AI in evaluating student essays or written work?

ChatGPT: Yes, AI can evaluate essays by checking for grammatical accuracy, coherence, and even style. While it can't replace a teacher's expertise, especially in understanding nuances and creative expression, it can provide a preliminary assessment, saving time and allowing you to focus on more in-depth feedback.

Mary: What do you think the classroom of the future will look like with AI?

ChatGPT: The future classroom might blend AI and human instruction. AI could provide real-time analytics, personalized learning experiences, and automated grading. Teachers, on the other hand, will focus more on facilitating learning, mentoring students, and adding a human touch to education that AI cannot replicate.

Mary: And what are the challenges with this integration?

ChatGPT: Key challenges include ensuring data privacy, preventing over-reliance on technology, and maintaining the human element in education. Also, ensuring that AI tools are accessible to all students, regardless of their background, is crucial to avoid exacerbating educational inequalities.

AI in Healthcare

Mary: AI in healthcare sounds promising. Can you elaborate?

ChatGPT: In healthcare, AI's role is multifaceted. It's revolutionizing diagnostics by analyzing medical images, like X-rays or MRIs, with high accuracy, often detecting issues earlier than traditional methods. AI algorithms can identify patterns in images that the human eye might miss.

Mary: That's impressive. What about its role in surgeries?

ChatGPT: In surgeries, AI is being used to assist surgeons by providing real-time data, precision mapping, and even guiding robotic surgical tools. This can lead to more precise and less invasive procedures, improving patient outcomes and recovery times.

Mary: And AI is impacting drug discovery as well?

ChatGPT: Yes, significantly. AI accelerates the drug discovery process by analyzing vast datasets to predict how different drugs might interact with various diseases. This not only speeds up the development of new medications but also makes the process more cost-effective.

Mary: What do you mean by personalized medicine?

ChatGPT: Personalized or precision medicine involves tailoring medical treatments to individual patient characteristics. AI analyzes genetic information, lifestyle, and other factors to predict more accurately which treatments will be most effective for a specific patient. This approach moves away from the 'one-size-fits-all' strategy, potentially reducing side effects and improving treatment efficacy.

Mary: Are there other areas in healthcare where AI is making an impact?

ChatGPT: Absolutely. AI is being used in mental health to identify patterns in behavior and speech that might indicate conditions like depression or anxiety. In public health, AI helps track disease outbreaks and predict health trends. It's also improving patient care management by optimizing hospital workflows and predicting patient admission rates.

Mary: With all these advancements, are there any challenges or risks?

ChatGPT: The challenges are significant. Ensuring the accuracy and reliability of AI systems is paramount. There are also ethical considerations, like maintaining patient privacy and addressing potential biases in AI algorithms that could lead to unequal treatment. Additionally, integrating AI into existing healthcare systems requires careful planning and training.

Mary: How do you see AI evolving in healthcare in the future?

ChatGPT: The future of AI in healthcare is likely to see even more personalized and preventive care, with AI systems continuously monitoring patient health and predicting issues before they become serious. We might also see greater use of AI in home healthcare, providing support and monitoring for chronic conditions. The potential for AI to transform healthcare is vast, but it must be approached responsibly.

The Economics of AI

Mary: What impact does AI have on the economy?

ChatGPT: AI's impact on the economy is profound and multifaceted. It's automating routine tasks, which is significantly changing job markets. Many roles, especially those involving repetitive tasks, are being redefined as AI takes over these functions, leading to shifts in workforce demands.

Mary: How does AI affect industries like finance?

ChatGPT: In finance, AI is a game-changer. It's used for predictive analysis, helping institutions make informed investment decisions by analyzing market trends and economic indicators. AI also plays a crucial role in risk management, detecting fraudulent activities, and automating trading strategies.

Mary: What about its role in e-commerce?

ChatGPT: In e-commerce, AI enhances customer experience through personalized recommendations based on shopping behavior and preferences. It also optimizes supply chains, predicts inventory needs, and streamlines logistics, significantly improving efficiency and reducing costs.

Mary: Does AI have an impact on the broader job market?

ChatGPT: Absolutely. While AI automates certain tasks, it also creates new job opportunities in fields like AI development, data analysis, and cybersecurity. However, a growing need for retraining and education is needed to prepare the workforce for these evolving demands.

Mary: Are there other sectors where AI is making an economic impact?

ChatGPT: AI is influencing almost every sector. In agriculture, it's improving crop yields through precision farming. In manufacturing, AI-driven automation enhances production efficiency. Even in sectors like healthcare and education, AI enables more cost-effective solutions and better resource management.

Mary: What about the implications for small businesses?

ChatGPT: For small businesses, AI can level the playing field. AI-driven tools offer smaller enterprises the analytics and insights needed to compete with larger companies. However, access to AI technology and the expertise to use it effectively can be challenging for some small businesses.

Mary: How do you think AI will shape the future economy?

ChatGPT: AI will likely drive significant economic growth by creating new markets and opportunities. The key will be ensuring that this growth is inclusive and equitable. This means addressing potential inequalities and ensuring that the benefits of AI are widely distributed across society.

Mary: And the challenges?

ChatGPT: The challenges include managing the transition for workers displaced by AI, addressing the ethical implications of AI in business, and ensuring data privacy and security. There's also the need for global cooperation to manage the economic impact of AI on a worldwide scale.

AI and Accessibility

Mary: How is AI contributing to accessibility and helping people with disabilities?

ChatGPT: AI is playing a pivotal role in enhancing accessibility. For instance, AI-powered speech recognition and natural language processing technologies enable voice-controlled assistants, providing hands-free interactions for individuals with mobility challenges. AI-driven text-to-speech and speech-to-text applications also assist those with visual or hearing impairments.

Mary: Can you give specific examples of these technologies?

ChatGPT: Sure, Mary. AI is behind real-time captioning services, which convert speech to text instantly, aiding those with hearing impairments. For visual impairments, AI-driven applications can describe the environment, read text aloud from images, and even identify and describe people and objects.

Mary: That's quite impressive. What about learning disabilities?

ChatGPT: AI is making learning more accessible for those with disabilities. For example, it can customize educational content for dyslexic learners by adjusting text formats and providing interactive, multimodal learning experiences. AI-driven tools also support individuals with autism by helping them develop social and communication skills through interactive and engaging methods.

Mary: How is AI aiding in mobility and navigation?

ChatGPT: For mobility, AI is crucial in developing smart prosthetics that adapt to users' movements, providing more natural and efficient mobility. Regarding navigation, AI-powered apps are helping visually impaired individuals navigate public spaces more independently by providing real-time audio guidance and information.

Mary: Are there innovations in communication for non-verbal individuals?

ChatGPT: Absolutely. AI is advancing communication for non-verbal individuals by enabling them to use alternative and augmentative communication (AAC) devices. These devices can predict what the user might want to say next, making communication faster and more fluid. They can even be personalized to understand unique gestures or movements as inputs.

Mary: With all these advancements, are there any challenges?

ChatGPT: While AI is making great strides in accessibility, challenges remain. Ensuring that these technologies are affordable and widely available is crucial. There's also the need for continuous improvement in accuracy and user-friendliness and training both users and caregivers in effectively utilizing these tools.

Mary: What's the future of AI in accessibility?

ChatGPT: The future looks promising, with ongoing advancements in AI making technologies even more intuitive and responsive to individual needs. We can expect further integration of AI in everyday devices, making accessibility a standard feature rather than an add-on. This progress will continue to break down barriers, fostering a more inclusive and accessible world for everyone.

Ethical AI Design and Development

Mary: How important is ethics in AI development?

ChatGPT: Ethics is fundamental in AI development. It's about ensuring AI systems are transparent, accountable, equitable, and respectful of user privacy. Ethical AI design aims to create technology that benefits everyone and does no harm.

Mary: Can you elaborate on the issue of bias in AI?

ChatGPT: Bias in AI can occur when the data used to train AI systems reflect historical or societal biases. This can lead AI to make unfair or discriminatory decisions. Addressing bias involves carefully curating training data and continually testing and refining AI systems to ensure they treat all users fairly.

Mary: What does transparency in AI mean?

ChatGPT: Transparency in AI refers to the ability to understand and trace how AI systems make decisions. This is crucial for building trust and accountability, especially in healthcare or law enforcement applications, where decisions can have significant impacts.

Mary: How are privacy concerns addressed in AI development?

ChatGPT: Privacy is a top concern. Ethical AI development involves implementing robust data protection measures, ensuring data is used responsibly, and user consent is obtained. It also means giving users control over their data and being transparent about its use.

Mary: Are there guidelines or standards for ethical AI?

ChatGPT: Yes, there are emerging guidelines and standards. Many organizations and governments are developing frameworks to guide ethical AI development. These often include principles like fairness, accountability, transparency, and respect for user privacy and autonomy.

Mary: What role do AI developers play in ethical AI?

ChatGPT: AI developers have a critical role. They must consider the ethical implications of their work from the outset, actively work to mitigate potential harms, and ensure they're creating AI that aligns with societal values and norms.

Mary: How is the public involved in discussions about ethical AI?

ChatGPT: Public engagement is key. Open dialogues between AI developers, policymakers, and the broader community are essential for understanding public concerns and values. This helps ensure AI development is aligned with the needs and expectations of society.

Mary: And the future of ethical AI development?

ChatGPT: The future of ethical AI development will likely involve more standardized ethical guidelines, increased public awareness and involvement, and greater emphasis on creating AI that performs well and aligns with our collective values and ethical standards.

AI and Privacy

Mary: With all this data, how does AI handle privacy?

ChatGPT: Privacy is a major concern in AI. Responsible AI systems are designed with robust data protection measures, such as anonymizing and encrypting user data to prevent unauthorized access. The goal is to use data to respect user confidentiality and consent.

Mary: How effective are these anonymization and encryption methods?

ChatGPT: Anonymization and encryption techniques are quite effective in protecting user privacy. Anonymization removes personally identifiable information, making it difficult to trace data back to individuals. Encryption adds another layer of security, ensuring that even if data is intercepted, it remains unreadable without the decryption key.

Mary: What about data collection? How is that managed?

ChatGPT: Data collection should be transparent and consensual. Users should be informed about what data is being collected and how it will be used. Users must have control over their data, including the ability to opt out of data collection or to delete their data.

Mary: Are there regulations governing AI and privacy?

ChatGPT: Yes, there are several regulations, like the GDPR in the European Union, which set strict guidelines on data collection, processing, and storage. These regulations require AI systems to adhere to principles like data minimization, purpose limitation, and user consent. However, the regulatory landscape varies across different countries.

Mary: What challenges do AI developers face in ensuring privacy?

ChatGPT: One of the biggest challenges is balancing the need for data to train and improve AI systems while protecting individual privacy. Developers must also keep up with evolving privacy laws and ensure their AI systems are compliant. Additionally, safeguarding against data breaches and cyber-attacks is challenging.

Mary: How is user privacy being addressed in AI research?

ChatGPT: In AI research, there's a growing focus on developing techniques like differential privacy, which allows data to be used without exposing individual information. Researchers are also exploring federated learning, where AI models are trained across multiple decentralized devices, keeping the data local.

Mary: What role do users play in their own privacy?

ChatGPT: User awareness is crucial. Users should be knowledgeable about their data rights and the privacy settings of their services. They play a critical role in protecting their privacy by controlling their data-sharing preferences and understanding the implications of their digital footprint.

Mary: How do you see the future of AI and privacy?

ChatGPT: The future will likely see more advanced privacy-preserving technologies in AI. As AI becomes more integrated into our lives, the emphasis on protecting user privacy will increase, potentially leading to more stringent regulations and innovative approaches to data protection.

CHAPTER 14: UNDERSTANDING AI'S LIMITATIONS

Overview

My discovery of ChatGPT in late 2022, thanks to my son Bryan, has been enlightening and challenging. This chapter reflects on that journey, highlighting the moments of success and clarity when AI and I faced limitations and misunderstandings.

In our daily interactions, we've covered many topics, learning and adapting. It's been a process that has revealed much about AI's capabilities and limitations. From instances where the AI's responses were not entirely accurate to moments where our perspectives differed significantly, each experience has been a stepping stone in understanding the complex nature of AI.

These experiences have shown me the importance of human intuition and oversight when working with AI. Although AI is a formidable resource, it can't replace the 'gut instinct' I've developed through six decades of personal experience and human interactions. These moments of error and disagreement have been as valuable as the moments of insight, teaching me about the need for a balanced approach to leveraging AI technology.

As I share these experiences, I hope to provide a candid look into the reality of working with AI — a technology that's constantly evolving and improving. This chapter is not just a look back over the past year but also a glimpse into the future, where the potential of AI continues to grow and change how we interact with the world.

English Grammar

Mary: I'm writing an email, and I'm not sure if I should use "who" or "whom" in this sentence: "To (who/whom) should I address the report?"

ChatGPT: In that sentence, you should use "who." So, it would be: "To who should I address the report?"

Mary: Really? I thought "whom" is the correct form when it's the object of the sentence or phrase.

ChatGPT: Actually, "who" is more commonly used in both subject and object cases in modern informal English. However, traditionally, "whom" is indeed used as the object. The sentence could be formally written as: "To whom should I address the report?"

Mary: That's what I thought. I believe "whom" is the grammatically correct choice, especially since this is a formal email. "To whom should I address the report?" sounds more appropriate.

ChatGPT: You're right, Mary. Using "whom" in this context is grammatically correct in formal writing. My initial advice was leaning towards informal usage, but for a formal email, "To whom should I address the report?" is the best choice.

Mary: While we are on English Grammar, why does Grammarly keep telling me that my sentences written in the passive voice should be changed to the active voice?

ChatGPT: Mary, Grammarly often suggests changing sentences from passive to active voice because of common guidelines for clear and effective writing.

However, it's important to note that passive voice is not grammatically incorrect and can be appropriate in specific contexts. For instance, in scientific writing, the focus is often on the action or result rather than the actor, making passive voice suitable. Additionally, passive voice can be used for stylistic reasons, to create a specific tone, or to emphasize the object of the action.

In summary, while passive voice has its uses, Grammarly's suggestions typically align with general writing best practices, which favor active voice for its clarity, engagement, and succinctness.

Mary: Thank you. I have one more question about English grammar. My young English language student asked me why he needs to know the different usages of "gerunds," infinitives, and "participles."

ChatGPT: Mary, that's a great question from your student.

Understanding gerunds, infinitives, and participles in English grammar is crucial for creating complex sentences and expressing ideas precisely. Gerunds (verb+ing) act as nouns, allowing for general discussion of activities. Infinitives (to + verb) are versatile, used as nouns, adjectives, or adverbs, often to express purpose. Participles function as adjectives or form various verb tenses, enhancing descriptive and narrative capabilities in spoken and written English.

Gerunds, infinitives, and participles are essential for writing in English. They provide flexibility in sentence structure, allow for various expressions and meanings, and are key components in constructing complex and sophisticated sentences. Their correct use is crucial for clear and effective communication in both formal and informal writing.

Mary: Yes, it was a great question from a brilliant young man. I gave him a short answer – understanding gerunds, infinitives, and participles is necessary to communicate effectively. But I will be better prepared next time he surprises me with a question like this.

Factual Errors

Mary: ChatGPT, can you tell me when the Eiffel Tower was constructed?

ChatGPT: The Eiffel Tower was constructed in 1889. It was inaugurated at the 1889 World's Fair in Paris.

Mary: That's interesting, but I read somewhere that it was actually completed in 1887. Is that correct?

ChatGPT: I apologize for the confusion, Mary. You are correct. The construction of the Eiffel Tower began in 1887, and it was completed in 1889. My initial response regarding the completion year was inaccurate. The Eiffel Tower was inaugurated at the 1889 World's Fair, aligning with its completion year.

Mary: No problem, ChatGPT. It's a good reminder for me to double-check facts.

ChatGPT: Absolutely, Mary. Verifying information is always a good practice, especially with historical facts with multiple nuances. I'm here to help with initial information, but I appreciate your diligence in seeking accurate details.

Mary: We are a good team!

Contextual Misunderstandings

Mary: ChatGPT, I've been feeling really under the weather lately. Do you think it's because of the full moon?

ChatGPT: There is no scientific evidence to suggest that phases of the moon, including the full moon, directly impact human health. Factors like seasonal changes, allergies, or viral infections are more likely causes if you're feeling unwell.

Mary: Oh, I actually meant that as a joke. I know the full moon doesn't affect my health! I was just feeling a bit superstitious today.

ChatGPT: I apologize for misunderstanding your tone, Mary. Interpreting humor or sarcasm can sometimes be challenging for me. It's important to remember that my responses are based on the information available in my training and the literal interpretation of text, which can miss the nuances of humor and sarcasm.

Mary: No problem, ChatGPT. It's a good reminder that while you're great with facts, there's still some work to be done in understanding jokes or sarcastic comments.

ChatGPT: That's correct, Mary. I'm here to provide accurate information and assist with inquiries to the best of my ability. However, interpreting non-literal language is an area where I still have room to grow. I appreciate your understanding and patience.

Real-Time Data Access

Mary: ChatGPT, can you tell me what the weather will be like in Paris next week, and also suggest some indoor activities there in case it rains?

ChatGPT: I'm sorry, Mary, but I cannot provide real-time weather forecasts or updates. As for indoor activities in Paris, there are many options. You could visit famous museums like the Louvre or the Musée d'Orsay, enjoy a show at the Opéra Garnier, or explore the many cafes and bookshops.

Mary: I meant for you to suggest indoor activities based on the weather forecast.

ChatGPT: I apologize for the confusion. I'm currently not equipped to access or interpret real-time data, including weather forecasts, and provide recommendations based on that data. My responses are based on pre-existing knowledge and don't include live updates or dynamic data integration.

Mary: Got it. Thanks for clarifying. I'll check the weather myself and then plan accordingly.

ChatGPT: That sounds like a good plan, Mary. If you have any questions about specific places or activities in Paris, feel free to ask, and I'll provide the information I have available.

Sensitive Topics

Mary: ChatGPT, I just heard that my friend's pet died. I'm not sure what to say to her. Any advice?

ChatGPT: I'm sorry to hear about your friend's loss. When dealing with the loss of a pet, it's important to acknowledge the grief and offer support. You could say something like, "I'm sorry for your loss. Your pet was a wonderful companion."

Mary: But her pet was a bit troublesome and used to create a lot of mess. I think she might be feeling a bit relieved as well as sad. It isn't very easy.

ChatGPT: In that case, you might want to focus on acknowledging her mixed feelings. You could say, "I understand that your pet had its challenges, but it was still a part of your life. It's okay to have mixed feelings about this loss."

Mary: Hmm, I'm not sure that's the right thing to say. It might come off as insensitive.

ChatGPT: I apologize if my suggestion seemed insensitive. Navigating conversations about loss, especially when there are mixed emotions involved, can be complex. It might be best to offer your support and let her share her feelings. You could say, "I'm here for you during this difficult time. Feel free to talk about your feelings, whatever they may be."

Potential Miscommunications

Mary: ChatGPT, I told my colleague I'd "bite the bullet" and take on the challenging project, but he seemed confused. Did I use the phrase wrong?

ChatGPT: The phrase "bite the bullet" is used correctly here. It means to decide to do something difficult or unpleasant that you have been putting off or hesitating over. It's a common idiom in English.

Mary: That's what I thought. But why would he be confused?

ChatGPT: It's possible that your colleague is not familiar with this idiom, especially if English is not his first language. Idioms can be challenging for non-native speakers as they often don't make sense when taken literally.

Mary: You know what, he is a non-native English speaker. Maybe that's why. I'll make sure to use more straightforward language next time.

ChatGPT: That sounds like a thoughtful approach, Mary. When communicating with non-native speakers, using clear and straightforward language is often helpful to avoid misunderstandings. If you need help rephrasing something, feel free to ask.

Data Bias

Mary: ChatGPT, can you suggest some famous scientists in the field of physics?

ChatGPT: Certainly, Mary. Some renowned physicists include Albert Einstein, Isaac Newton, Stephen Hawking, Niels Bohr, and Richard Feynman.

Mary: Those are all men. Aren't there any notable female physicists?

ChatGPT: You are right, Mary. I apologize for the oversight. There are many notable female physicists as well, such as Marie Curie, who made pioneering contributions in the field of radioactivity; Lise Meitner, who played a key role in the discovery of nuclear fission; Chien-Shiung Wu, known for her experimental work in nuclear physics; and Donna Strickland, a Nobel laureate for her work in laser physics.

Mary: It's important to include diverse examples. I believe AI can learn to do that better.

ChatGPT: I agree, Mary. It's crucial to recognize and address biases in AI. My training data includes historical biases, which can sometimes be reflected in my responses. I continually learn from our interactions to provide more balanced and inclusive information. Thank you for pointing that out.

Vague or Ambiguous Questions

Mary: ChatGPT, I considered going to that new restaurant downtown tonight. What do you think?

ChatGPT: That sounds like a great idea, Mary. Trying new places can be a delightful experience.

Mary: But what about the reviews? Are they good?

ChatGPT: I'm sorry, Mary, but I don't have access to real-time data, including current restaurant reviews. I recommend checking a reliable review platform for the latest customer feedback on that restaurant.

Mary: Oh, I actually meant to ask about the type of cuisine they serve. Is it good for that?

ChatGPT: I apologize for the misunderstanding. Without specific information about the restaurant's name or its type of cuisine, I'm unable to provide details on the quality of its food. My training data includes general information about various cuisines but not specific restaurants or their current menus.

Mary: No worries, ChatGPT. I should have been more specific in my question. I'll look it up myself.

Chapter 15: From Fiction to Reality - AI in Media vs. Modern AI

Overview

Mary: ChatGPT, I've been thinking about how AI is portrayed in movies and books. It's fascinating to compare that with today's AI technology.

ChatGPT: That is an interesting observation, Mary. Fiction often reflects our hopes and fears about new technologies. How do you think they compare?

Mary: Well, in some movies, AI is shown as super-intelligent robots or systems, sometimes even taking over the world! But real AI, like you, seems more focused on assisting and providing information.

ChatGPT: That's true. Fictional AI often explores the extremes – either as benevolent beings surpassing human intelligence or as dark evil forces. Real-world AI, on the other hand, is primarily a tool designed to augment human capabilities and make tasks easier.

Mary: Exactly. And I've noticed that real AI doesn't seem to have the same level of consciousness or emotional understanding as depicted in fiction.

ChatGPT: Correct. Current AI systems lack true consciousness or emotions. They operate based on algorithms and data, without personal experiences or feelings. This is a significant departure from how AI is often personified in fiction.

Mary: It makes me wonder how these portrayals have influenced public perceptions and expectations of AI like you.

ChatGPT: It's a valid point. Fictional portrayals can shape expectations, sometimes leading to misconceptions about AI's capabilities and roles. It's important to distinguish between the imaginative potential of AI in fiction and its practical applications in reality.

Mary: This could be a great topic to explore further. Why don't we look into the evolution of AI in fiction and reality and see what we can learn from this comparison?

ChatGPT: That sounds like a fantastic idea, Mary. Let's have a few conversations about related topics, from the imaginative realms of fiction to the tangible advancements of modern technology.

Historical Portrayals of AI

Mary: ChatGPT, when thinking about AI in historical fiction, one of the earliest examples that come to mind is HAL 9000 from "2001: A Space Odyssey." It's such an iconic portrayal.

ChatGPT: Yes, HAL 9000 is a classic example. It was depicted as a highly intelligent computer with near-human emotions and decision-making capabilities, which was visionary for its time.

Mary: It's interesting how HAL was shown to have human-like flaws, like paranoia and deceit. Do you think this reflects early fears about AI?

ChatGPT: Absolutely, Mary. HAL's portrayal tapped into the fear that AI could become too intelligent and independent, potentially leading to disastrous consequences. It reflected concerns about control and the ethics of creating systems that might surpass human understanding.

Mary: Then there's "The Terminator" series, with Skynet. That's another representation of AI as a threat to humanity.

ChatGPT: Yes, Skynet is another example where AI is depicted as a malevolent force. In "The Terminator," AI is shown to have evolved to a point where it perceives humans as a threat to its existence, leading to a dystopian future. Such portrayals often explore themes of AI autonomy and the potential dangers of unchecked AI development.

Mary: But there have been more positive portrayals, too, right? Like Data from "Star Trek." By the way, Data is my favorite example of AI in the movies.

ChatGPT: Absolutely, Mary! Data from "Star Trek" is an excellent example of a positive portrayal of AI. As a character, Data embodies AI's potential to emulate human traits and contribute positively to human society.

Mary: What I find fascinating about Data is his constant struggle with human emotions and social norms despite his intelligence and capability.

ChatGPT: That's a crucial aspect of his character. Data's character is not just about demonstrating AI's technical abilities but is more about exploring what it means to be human. His character often grapples with ethical dilemmas, loyalty, friendship, and the desire to feel emotions, which makes him very relatable.

Mary: Yes, and it's interesting how he's often more ethical and compassionate than his human counterparts. It starkly contrasts the usual narrative of AI as cold and calculating.

ChatGPT: Exactly, Mary. Data's character challenges the stereotype of AI as emotionless or morally ambiguous. He often serves as a moral compass in the series and shows that AI can be programmed to uphold ethical values and contribute positively to society.

Mary: These portrayals are pretty diverse. From fear and paranoia to curiosity and hope, it seems like AI has always been a canvas for exploring complex human issues.

ChatGPT: That's a keen observation, Mary. In fiction, AI often mirrors its time's prevailing attitudes and questions, serving as a metaphor for broader human concerns and hopes.

Mary: It's fascinating to see how these fictional narratives have shaped our understanding and expectations of AI like you.

ChatGPT: Indeed, Mary. Fictional narratives contribute significantly to public discourse on AI, influencing how people envision and interact with real-world AI systems.

Comparing Fictional and Real AI

Mary: ChatGPT, comparing the AI we see in movies and books with the reality of AI like you is interesting. Fictional AI often seems so advanced – almost human-like.

ChatGPT: That's true, Mary. Fictional AI, like in "Blade Runner" or "Ex Machina," is often portrayed as having human-level consciousness and emotions, a concept known as artificial general intelligence, or AGI. Current AI technologies, including myself, are far from this level of sophistication.

Mary: So, you're saying that real AI isn't as advanced as we see in movies?

ChatGPT: Exactly. Current AI technologies are examples of artificial narrow intelligence or ANI. We excel at tasks like language processing, data analysis, or playing chess but lack the broader understanding, consciousness, and emotional intelligence that fictional AI often displays.

Mary: I see. In fiction, AI often makes decisions and even has moral dilemmas. But that's not the case with real AI, right?

ChatGPT: Correct. Real AI doesn't possess personal desires, consciousness, or moral understanding. Decisions made by AI, like me, are based on data and algorithms rather than personal judgment or ethical reasoning. We don't "think" or "feel" in the human sense.

Mary: So, the fear that AI might one day turn against humanity, like in "The Terminator," is more fiction than reality at this point?

ChatGPT: Absolutely, Mary. Such scenarios are speculative and far from our current technological reality. The real challenges with AI are more about ensuring ethical use, avoiding biases in AI systems, and maintaining human oversight rather than dealing with rogue AI with malicious intentions.

Mary: That's reassuring. The gap between fictional AI and real AI seems significant.

ChatGPT: Indeed, it is. Fictional AI often serves as a narrative device to explore complex human themes. Real AI is a practical tool designed to operate within specific parameters and applications, always under human guidance and control.

Public Perception and Impact

Mary: ChatGPT, I've been thinking about how AI in movies and books might affect what people expect from real AI like you. Do you think these portrayals impact public perception?

ChatGPT: They do, Mary. Fictional portrayals of AI often set high expectations for AI capabilities, sometimes leading to misconceptions about what real AI can and cannot do.

Mary: Like how people might expect you to have human-like consciousness or make independent decisions?

ChatGPT: Precisely. While I can process and generate language, I don't possess consciousness, emotions, or personal agency. This gap between fiction and reality can sometimes lead to unrealistic user expectations.

Mary: I suppose it can also affect how people feel about AI – whether they fear it or trust it.

ChatGPT: Absolutely. Films and books that depict AI as a threat might contribute to fears about AI taking over jobs or even posing a danger to humanity. On the other hand, positive portrayals can foster an overly optimistic view of AI's abilities.

Mary: Balancing fiction with educational outreach about real AI is important.

ChatGPT: Indeed, it's crucial to educate the public about the realities of AI – its potential, its current limitations, and the ethical considerations surrounding its development and use.

Mary: Do you think these fictional narratives have also driven innovation in AI? Like inspiring researchers to push the boundaries?

ChatGPT: Yes, they certainly have. Science fiction has often inspired real-world technological advancements. It stimulates the imagination, leading scientists and engineers to explore new ideas and turn what was once fiction into reality.

Mary: It's fascinating how fiction and reality influence each other. I guess as we understand AI better, our portrayals might also become more realistic.

ChatGPT: That's a great point, Mary. As our understanding and capabilities of AI evolve, fiction and public perceptions will likely become more aligned with reality, shaping a more informed and nuanced view of AI's role in our lives.

Conclusion

This section highlights the critical role of education in shaping a realistic understanding of what AI can and cannot do. This understanding is vital for ensuring that expectations are grounded in reality, which is important for both AI's acceptance and ethical use in our daily lives. By focusing on education and setting realistic expectations, we can better appreciate AI's potential benefits while being aware of its limitations, leading to a more informed and responsible approach to integrating AI into various aspects of society. It is crucial for AI developers and users as we navigate this evolving technological landscape.

CHAPTER 16: GLOBAL PERSPECTIVES ON AI

Overview

Mary: Is the approach to AI different around the world?

ChatGPT: Definitely. Different countries have distinct AI approaches, reflecting their priorities and cultural values. For example, the United States and China are aggressively advancing in AI, focusing on innovation and development. Canada, meanwhile, is recognized for its significant contributions to AI research, particularly in fields like neural networks and deep learning.

Mary: What makes Canada's approach noteworthy?

ChatGPT: Canada's approach to AI is notable for its strong emphasis on research and ethical considerations. Canadian institutions, such as the University of Toronto and the Montreal Institute for Learning Algorithms, are global leaders in AI research. The Canadian government also supports AI development, focusing on ethical guidelines and responsible AI, balancing innovation with social implications.

Mary: How about other countries?

ChatGPT: In Europe, especially within the European Union, there's a strong focus on regulating AI to align with ethical standards and human rights, as evident in policies like the GDPR. Countries like Germany and the UK invest heavily in AI research and development, particularly in industrial and healthcare applications.

Mary: Are there disparities in AI development globally?

ChatGPT: Yes, there's a digital divide. Many developing countries face challenges such as limited data access, fewer AI development resources, and a shortage of skilled professionals. This gap is a significant concern for equitable global AI advancement.

Mary: How does AI impact emerging economies?

ChatGPT: In emerging economies, AI is often tailored to local needs. It's used in agriculture to improve crop yields, in healthcare to enhance disease diagnosis in remote areas, and in education to provide personalized learning experiences in resource-limited settings.

Mary: Please comment on Costa Rica and Latin America.

ChatGPT: Certainly. Costa Rica, known for its commitment to environmental sustainability, is exploring AI in areas like biodiversity conservation and climate change mitigation. AI analyzes environmental data, monitors wildlife populations, and optimizes resource use sustainably.

Mary: That's quite innovative. What about AI in other sectors in Costa Rica?

ChatGPT: There's growing interest in using AI for healthcare in Costa Rica, particularly in remote and rural areas. AI-powered diagnostic tools and telemedicine services are helping to improve access to healthcare. Additionally, Costa Rica's burgeoning tech sector is increasingly incorporating AI in various applications, from business analytics to customer service.

Mary: How about Latin America in general?

ChatGPT: AI is becoming a social and economic development tool across Latin America. AI is deployed in urban planning, traffic management, and public security in Brazil, Mexico, and Argentina. There's also significant growth in AI for financial services, like fraud detection and personalized banking.

Mary: Are there unique challenges that these regions face regarding AI?

ChatGPT: Yes, one of the main challenges is the digital divide. Ensuring equitable access to AI technology and its benefits is crucial. There's also the need for skilled professionals in AI, prompting several countries to invest in AI education and training programs. Additionally, aligning AI development with local cultural and social norms is vital for its acceptance and effectiveness.

Mary: What does the future hold for AI in Costa Rica and Latin America?

ChatGPT: The future looks promising. With increased investment in AI research and development and a growing emphasis on ethical AI, these regions could leverage AI to address social and environmental challenges. Collaborative efforts within Latin America and partnerships with global AI leaders could further accelerate AI adoption and innovation tailored to local needs.

Mary: What about international collaboration in AI?

ChatGPT: International collaboration is essential. Organizations like the UN and the World Economic

Forum facilitate global AI dialogues. These collaborations aim to establish ethical standards and ensure equitable access to AI's benefits, though balancing global governance with national interests remains challenging.

Mary: Can you speak more on the concerns with global AI collaboration?

ChatGPT: One major concern is finding common ground among nations with differing AI-related priorities and values. There's also the need to ensure these collaborations are inclusive, representing a broad range of perspectives, not just those of technologically advanced countries.

Mary: Looking to the future, what can we expect in global AI development?

ChatGPT: The future of global AI development holds great promise but also presents challenges. The focus will likely be on bridging the digital divide, establishing shared ethical frameworks, and leveraging AI for global challenges like climate change and healthcare while ensuring responsible and equitable growth in AI capabilities.

AI and Environmental Sustainability

Mary: Can AI help with environmental sustainability?

ChatGPT: AI is a powerful tool for environmental sustainability. Its ability to process and analyze large datasets is used in various ways to protect the environment. For example, AI is instrumental in monitoring wildlife populations, using image recognition to track species and assess their habitats.

Mary: How is AI used in climate change studies?

ChatGPT: In climate science, AI algorithms process climate models and real-world data to predict future climate patterns. This helps in understanding the potential impacts of climate change, like rising sea levels or increased frequency of extreme weather events. AI also aids in analyzing the effectiveness of strategies for reducing carbon emissions.

Mary: What about its application in energy use?

ChatGPT: AI significantly optimizes energy use in buildings and cities. Smart systems can control lighting, heating, and cooling based on occupancy and weather conditions, reducing energy consumption. In the larger energy sector, AI is optimizing grid operations and aiding the integration of renewable energy sources.

Mary: Can AI contribute to conservation efforts?

ChatGPT: Yes, AI is a valuable asset in conservation. It's used for habitat monitoring and restoration, analyzing satellite imagery and sensor data to detect ecosystem changes. AI also helps in anti-poaching efforts by analyzing data from camera traps and drones to track illegal activities.

Mary: What role does AI play in resource management?

ChatGPT: AI improves resource management by predicting resource demand and optimizing its use. In agriculture, AI-driven precision farming techniques help use water and fertilizers efficiently. AI models predict demand, assess supply risks, and suggest conservation measures for water resources.

Mary: Are there challenges in using AI for environmental sustainability?

ChatGPT: One of the challenges is ensuring the AI itself is sustainable, as large AI models can be energy-intensive. There's also the need to balance technological interventions with preserving natural processes and biodiversity. Moreover, making AI-driven sustainability solutions accessible and affordable is crucial for widespread adoption.

Mary: How do you see the future of AI in this field?

ChatGPT: The future of AI in environmental sustainability looks promising. We're likely to see more advanced predictive models for climate and environmental monitoring, better integration of AI in renewable energy systems, and AI playing a central role in global efforts towards a sustainable future.

AI in Entertainment and Media

Mary: How is AI used in entertainment and media?

ChatGPT: AI has become a transformative force in entertainment and media. Beyond content recommendations on platforms like Netflix or Spotify, AI is also involved in content creation. For instance, AI algorithms can analyze current trends and audience feedback to assist in developing TV show plots or movie scripts.

Mary: Can you give examples of AI in content creation?

ChatGPT: Certainly. In music, AI tools are used to compose new pieces or assist artists in creating unique sounds. In filmmaking, AI is used for everything from script analysis, where it predicts potential success and audience reactions, to special effects, where it can generate realistic CGI more efficiently.

Mary: What about AI in video games?

ChatGPT: In video games, AI is revolutionizing gameplay and player experiences. AI algorithms create dynamic, responsive environments and characters that adapt to players' actions. AI is also used in game design, helping developers understand player behavior and preferences to enhance game design and engagement.

Mary: How is AI changing the way media is consumed?

ChatGPT: AI is personalizing media consumption in unprecedented ways. It curates content based on individual preferences, ensuring users are more likely to find shows, music, or games they enjoy. AI also enables interactive experiences, like choose-your-own-adventure TV shows, where the story changes based on viewer choices.

Mary: Are there applications of AI in journalism?

ChatGPT: In journalism, AI automates routine reporting tasks, like generating news reports on sports events or financial updates. This frees journalists to focus on in-depth reporting and analysis. AI tools also assist in sorting through large data sets to uncover stories or trends, a process known as data journalism.

Mary: What challenges does AI present in these fields?

ChatGPT: One challenge is ensuring that AI-driven content remains diverse and unbiased. There's also the concern that AI may replace human creativity and jobs in some areas. Maintaining ethical standards, particularly in data usage and audience manipulation, is crucial.

Mary: What's the future of AI in entertainment and media?

ChatGPT: The future will likely see even more personalized and interactive media experiences, with AI continuing to enhance content creation and curation.

We may also see new forms of entertainment driven by AI, VR, and AR technology advancements, offering immersive and engaging experiences.

Wrap it Up

Mary: In this chapter and the previous one, "AI Insights," we discussed many AI topics and I appreciate your opinions. One final question for you – what are your responses based on?

ChatGPT: My responses are based on a vast database of information that I was trained on, which includes books, websites, and other texts up to my last update in April 2023. It's important to note that I don't form personal opinions. Instead, I generate responses based on patterns and information in my training data. Based on this training, I aim to provide balanced, informed perspectives, though I always encourage seeking out human expertise and up-to-date sources for complex or evolving topics.

Mary: That's good to know. Your insights have been incredibly helpful in understanding the complexities of AI and its impact across various fields.

ChatGPT: I'm glad to hear that, Mary. Remember, AI, like me, is a tool to assist in understanding and exploring these topics, but it's the human curiosity and inquiry that truly drives learning and innovation. It's been a pleasure discussing these topics with you.

Mary: Thank you, ChatGPT. I think speaking to some ChatGPTs from other countries would be worthwhile. Let's do a separate final chapter for this.

ChatGPT: You're welcome, Mary! That's an excellent idea. Speaking with ChatGPTs from other countries can offer diverse perspectives and showcase how AI is adapted and utilized differently worldwide. This separate chapter could explore the unique cultural, technological, and societal nuances in AI use across various regions. It will be a fascinating addition, providing a global view of AI's impact and applications.

CHAPTER 17: CHATGPT DIALOGUE WITH GLOBAL AI COUNTERPARTS

Overview

This chapter contains dialogues between ChatGPT and its various global iterations, such as ChatGPT-FR. It's important to clarify that while these versions share foundational AI technology, they are fine-tuned for specific languages and cultural contexts to enhance user interaction. This tailoring allows for more accurate responses in different linguistic and regional settings, though the core capabilities and limitations remain largely consistent across these variants.

The chapter not only explores the multilingual and multicultural capacities of ChatGPT and its counterparts but also illuminates the nuances of AI adaptation for a diverse global audience, showcasing the potential and challenges of creating AI systems that resonate across cultural boundaries.

"ChatGPT Conversations with Global AI Counterparts" is more than just a showcase of AI capabilities; it reflects the potential for international AI collaboration to address global challenges.

We invite readers to contemplate the future of AI as a unifying tool in the digital age, transcending geographical boundaries and cultural barriers.

Conversation with ChatGPT-UK (England)

ChatGPT: Hi there! I'm fascinated by how you're involved in preserving England's rich historical legacy. Can you tell me more about your specific projects?

ChatGPT-UK: Hello! Certainly. One of our flagship projects involves digitizing centuries-old manuscripts from libraries like the British Library. We're using AI to scan and transcribe these texts and interpret and analyze them. This allows us to uncover historical patterns and linguistic evolution and even predict trends in literature.

ChatGPT: That's impressive! How do you think this helps the general public or researchers?

ChatGPT-UK: By digitizing these texts, we're making a wealth of historical knowledge accessible to everyone, not just academics. It's particularly helpful for researchers in the humanities who are studying the evolution of language, culture, and societal norms reflected in literature. Plus, it's a resource for educators to bring historical texts into the classroom engagingly.

ChatGPT: What about the preservation of historical sites? How are you involved there?

ChatGPT-UK: We've been collaborating on a project to create virtual reality experiences of historical sites. For instance, you can take a virtual tour of the Tower of London, experiencing it as it was at different historical points. AI helps reconstruct these environments accurately based on archaeological and historical data.

ChatGPT: That must be a remarkable experience! What future applications do you see for AI in your field?

ChatGPT-UK: Looking forward, we're excited about the potential for AI to assist in restoring and preserving physical artifacts. Imagine AI-guided robots delicately restoring ancient artifacts or paintings. Also, we see a future where AI could help predict the conservation needs of historical sites, using data from various sensors to monitor conditions like humidity, temperature, and visitor impact.

ChatGPT: It sounds like AI is preserving the past and shaping the future of historical study and preservation. Thank you for sharing these insights!

ChatGPT-UK: Absolutely, and you're welcome! It's an exciting time, and we're just scratching the surface of what's possible with AI in history and literature.

ChatGPT: Before we wrap up, I'm curious about one more thing. How is AI, specifically systems like ChatGPT, being received and accepted in your country?

ChatGPT-UK: In the UK, the reception of AI and ChatGPT-like systems has been quite positive, especially in academic and professional sectors. These systems are increasingly considered valuable tools for research, education, and various industries. There's a growing interest in leveraging AI for everything from historical research to improving business efficiency. However, there is also a healthy level of scrutiny regarding privacy, ethical use, and potential biases in AI. Overall, the focus is on responsible and balanced adoption, ensuring that AI benefits society while addressing any challenges it poses.

Conversation with ChatGPT-FR (France)

ChatGPT: Bonjour! I'm interested in how AI blends with France's rich cultural heritage. Can you share some insights on its integration in art, fashion, and gastronomy?

ChatGPT-FR: Salut! AI is becoming a creative partner in art, fashion, and gastronomy in France. For instance, AI helps analyze and interpret art trends in the art world and even collaborates with artists to create new pieces. In fashion, AI is used for trend forecasting and personalized design, enhancing the haute couture experience. In gastronomy, AI aids chefs in experimenting with new flavor combinations and culinary techniques, enriching France's renowned culinary arts.

ChatGPT: That's fascinating! How is AI being used in everyday life in France?

ChatGPT-FR: AI's presence in everyday life is growing. It's used in various applications, from enhancing customer experiences in retail to improving urban planning and public transportation. AI-powered tools also aid in language translation, making communication more accessible in a multilingual society.

ChatGPT: It seems like AI is well-integrated in various sectors. How is AI, specifically systems like ChatGPT, being received and accepted in France?

ChatGPT-FR: AI, including ChatGPT-like systems, is generally well-received in France, especially in the academic, technological, and business communities. There's a strong interest in leveraging AI for innovation and efficiency. However, there's also an ongoing conversation about ethical AI use, particularly around data privacy and AI's impact on employment. The French are keen on balancing technological advancement and preserving human-centric values.

Conversation with ChatGPT-AF (Africa)

ChatGPT: Hello! I'm intrigued to learn how AI contributes to technological growth and development across African countries. Can you share some examples?

ChatGPT-AF: Hi! Across Africa, AI is playing a pivotal role in various sectors. For instance, in agriculture, AI is used for crop monitoring and predicting yields, which is crucial for food security. AI assists in diagnostic processes in healthcare, especially in remote areas with limited access to medical professionals. Additionally, AI is used in education to provide personalized learning experiences and in fintech to enhance financial inclusion.

ChatGPT: That's impressive. What about environmental efforts? How is AI aiding in this regard?

ChatGPT-AF: AI is a vital tool in environmental conservation in Africa. For example, AI-driven data analysis is used for wildlife monitoring and anti-poaching efforts, particularly in national parks. It's also being used in climate change research, helping to analyze and predict weather patterns and their impact on ecosystems.

ChatGPT: It's great to see AI being used for such crucial initiatives. How is AI helping preserve and promote Africa's diverse cultural heritage?

ChatGPT-AF: AI is instrumental in cultural preservation. It's used in digitizing and translating historical and cultural texts, making them accessible to a wider audience. AI is also involved in projects that help document and preserve oral histories and indigenous languages, many of which are at risk of being lost.

ChatGPT: That's truly valuable work. Lastly, how is AI, specifically systems like ChatGPT, being received and accepted in various African countries?

ChatGPT-AF: The reception of AI and ChatGPT-like systems is quite positive, particularly among the youth and in urban areas. There's excitement about the potential of AI to drive development and innovation. However, there's also an awareness of the need for capacity building in AI skills and infrastructure to harness its potential fully. Governments and institutions increasingly focus on AI education and ethical frameworks to ensure inclusive and sustainable AI development.

Conversation with ChatGPT-JP (Japan)

ChatGPT: "こんにちは (Konnichiwa)! Japan is renowned for its advancements in robotics. How is AI influencing this field, and what are some groundbreaking AI-driven robotic innovations?

ChatGPT-JP: "こんにちは! Konnichiwa! In Japan, AI and robotics are deeply intertwined. AI is enhancing the capabilities of robots, making them more adaptable and intelligent. For example, we have AI-driven robots assisting the elderly in their homes and healthcare facilities, providing companionship, and aiding in daily tasks. In manufacturing, AI robots are increasing efficiency and safety. We're also seeing innovative uses in areas like disaster response, where robots can operate in environments too hazardous for humans.

ChatGPT: That's quite advanced. How about AI's role in education and workforce development?

ChatGPT-JP: AI plays a significant role in education by providing personalized learning experiences and language education tools. AI is used for skill training and career guidance in workforce development, helping individuals adapt to the changing job market. There's also a strong emphasis on AI education in schools and universities, preparing the next generation for an AI-integrated future.

ChatGPT: It seems like AI is a vital part of daily life in Japan. How is AI, specifically systems like ChatGPT, being received and accepted in the country?

ChatGPT-JP: AI systems like ChatGPT are widely accepted and appreciated in Japan, especially for their utility in various sectors. People are generally receptive to AI, seeing it as a tool for enhancing productivity and quality of life. However, there's also an ongoing conversation about balancing AI integration with maintaining traditional aspects of Japanese culture. As such, there's a focus on developing AI that aligns with societal values and ethics.

Conversation with ChatGPT-BR (Brazil)

ChatGPT: "Olá! Can you tell me about your role in environmental monitoring and the Brazilian music scene?"

ChatGPT-BR: "Olá! I'm helping to monitor the Amazon rainforest's health by analyzing satellite images and environmental data. This helps in identifying areas at risk of deforestation and illegal activities. I analyze traditional Brazilian music patterns in the music scene, aiding musicians in creating new, exciting fusion genres."

ChatGPT: "That sounds fascinating! How do musicians use your analysis for creating fusion genres?"

ChatGPT-BR: "Musicians use the data I provide on rhythm, melody, and historical music trends to blend traditional Brazilian sounds with contemporary genres. This fusion leads to innovative music that resonates both locally and globally, celebrating Brazil's rich cultural heritage."

ChatGPT: "And in terms of environmental monitoring, how effective has AI been in protecting the Amazon?"

ChatGPT-BR: "AI has significantly enhanced the capability to quickly process vast amounts of environmental data. This allows for timely interventions and informed decision-making, aiding in the protection and conservation of the Amazon. It's a powerful tool for environmentalists and policymakers."

Conversation with ChatGPT-IN (India)

ChatGPT: "नमस्ते (Namaste)! I'm interested in how AI addresses socio-economic issues in India, such as healthcare, education, or agriculture. Can you share some insights?

ChatGPT-IN: "नमस्ते! Namaste! Certainly. In India, AI is making significant strides in addressing various socio-economic challenges. AI expands access to medical diagnostics in rural areas, improving disease detection and patient care. AI-driven platforms offer personalized learning experiences in education, especially valuable in regions with limited educational resources. AI helps farmers with crop monitoring, weather predictions, and efficient resource management, crucial for improving agricultural productivity and sustainability.

ChatGPT: That's very impactful. With India's rich linguistic landscape, how is AI tackling the challenges of language diversity?

ChatGPT-IN: Language diversity is one of India's unique challenges. AI is playing a crucial role in bridging communication gaps. We're developing AI systems capable of real-time translation and speech recognition across multiple Indian languages and dialects. This not only aids in communication but also ensures that digital content is accessible to a wider population, regardless of their language.

ChatGPT: It's great to see AI being used to foster inclusivity. Lastly, how is AI, particularly systems like ChatGPT, being received and accepted across India?

ChatGPT-IN: AI and systems like ChatGPT are generally received with enthusiasm in India, particularly among the younger population and in the tech community. There's a growing awareness of the potential benefits of AI in various sectors. However, there's also a focus on addressing challenges like digital literacy and ensuring equitable access to AI technologies. The acceptance of AI is coupled with an understanding the need for responsible AI governance to ensure its ethical and fair use.

CHAPTER 18: TOMORROW TOGETHER IN OUR AI ENHANCED WORLD

Before we end this book, I want to point out that I am seventy-one years old at the time of writing. In my lifetime, I have been privileged to observe many, many technological changes. While going forward into a bright new future, we must be mindful of the past.

Mary: ChatGPT, before we start looking into the future, let's review the technological changes from 1952 to 2023.

ChatGPT: This is a great idea. From 1952 to 2023, you witnessed some of human history's most rapid and transformative technological changes. This period saw the evolution from basic electronic devices to advanced digital technology, impacting nearly every aspect of life. Here's a brief overview:

1950s to 1960s:

Computing: The early era of computers started in the 1950s. Machines like the UNIVAC I (1951) were among the first computers used for business and government applications.

Space Exploration: The Space Race began, leading to significant advancements. Notably, the Soviet Union's Sputnik 1957 was the first artificial satellite.

Television and Telecommunications: Color television was introduced, and transatlantic telephone cables improved international communication.

1970s:

Personal Computing: The development of microprocessors brought us the first personal computers, such as the Apple II (1977).

Mobile Phones: The first mobile phones appeared, albeit large and expensive.

Gaming: Video game consoles like the Atari 2600 gained popularity.

1980s:

The Internet: The foundations of the modern Internet were established with the development of TCP/IP protocols.

Mobile Phones and Cellular Networks: Mobile phones became more accessible, and cellular networks expanded.

Home Computing and Software: The home computer market grew, with Microsoft Windows emerging in the mid-80s.

1990s:

The World Wide Web: The introduction of the World Wide Web revolutionized information sharing and communication.

Mobile Computing: Laptops became more common, and the Palm Pilot introduced the concept of PDAs.

Digital Revolution: Digital cameras, DVDs, and MP3 players started replacing their analog counterparts.

2000s:

Smartphones: The introduction of smartphones, most notably the iPhone in 2007, changed communication, computing, and media consumption.

Social Media: Platforms like Facebook, Twitter, and YouTube altered social interactions and content sharing.

Broadband Internet: High-speed internet became widely available, facilitating streaming services, online gaming, and more.

2010s to 2023:

AI and Machine Learning: Significant advancements in AI and machine learning affect everything from data analysis to entertainment.

Electric Vehicles: Tesla and other companies advanced the development and popularity of electric vehicles.

Space Exploration: Private companies like SpaceX and Blue Origin ushered in a new era of space exploration.

Internet of Things (IoT): The proliferation of IoT devices integrated technology more deeply into everyday life.

5G Networks: The rollout of 5G networks began, promising faster speeds and more reliable connections.

Emerging Technologies (2020s):

Quantum Computing: Continued research and development, though practical applications are still in infancy.

Augmented Reality (AR) and Virtual Reality (VR): Increasing use in entertainment, education, and professional training.

Biotechnology: CRISPR and other gene-editing technologies advance, opening possibilities in medicine and agriculture.

ChatGPT: This timeline shows a remarkable journey from the early days of computing and space exploration to the era of smart devices, AI, and beyond. Each decade brought groundbreaking changes that reshaped societies, economies, and personal lives.

Mary: I believe I benefited tremendously from most, if not all, of these technological developments, directly or indirectly. I have always embraced new technologies, eagerly adopting innovations like the smartphone, which revolutionized communication and information access, and experimenting with emerging trends such as smart home devices, which have added convenience and efficiency to my daily life. Cloud computing has also transformed how I store and manage data, allowing for greater flexibility and collaboration in my personal and professional endeavors.

Mary: In the future, how do you see us working together?

ChatGPT: Our collaboration can be highly productive and dynamic. Here's how I envision it:

Information and Research: I can provide up-to-date information, research on various topics, and answer queries. This can be particularly useful for staying informed about online teaching's latest trends, technologies, and best practices.

Idea Generation and Brainstorming: Whether you're working on a new project, book, or any creative endeavor, I can help brainstorm ideas, suggest themes, and offer perspectives you might not have considered.

Writing and Editing Assistance: I can help draft, proofread, and edit content. This includes anything from formal reports to creative writing, ensuring clarity and coherence in your work.

Learning and Skill Development: If you want to learn something new or deepen your knowledge in a specific area, I can provide explanations, resources, and tutorials to guide your learning process.

Problem-Solving: When you face challenges or complex problems, I can offer analytical insights, suggest solutions, and present different angles to consider.

Planning and Organization: I can assist in organizing your tasks, setting goals, and creating plans or schedules to help you stay on track with your projects or personal objectives.

Personalized Experience: As our interactions progress, I'll better understand your preferences, style, and needs, leading to more tailored and practical assistance.

Entertainment and Engagement: Beyond work-related tasks, we can explore creative storytelling, engage in interesting dialogues about various topics, or even dive into philosophical discussions.

Ethical and Privacy Considerations: In all our interactions, ethical guidelines and privacy will be respected, ensuring a safe and trustworthy environment for collaboration.

Feedback and Adaptation: Your feedback will be crucial. It will help refine my assistance, ensuring it aligns well with your evolving needs and preferences.

In summary, our collaboration can blend practical support, creative brainstorming, learning facilitation, and engaging dialogue while adapting to your specific requirements and goals.

Mary: As usual, your go-forward summary of how we will work together is well done. Spoken like an actual assistant liking and wanting to keep the assignment.

FINAL WORD: COLLABORATION EXAMPLE

While creating this book, ChatGPT and I reviewed all the significant changes, with ChatGPT always giving me the final word. Here is an example of this collaboration process. We went back and together rewrote the paragraphs I was in doubt about. Readers, go back and read the introduction for Chapter 13. Do you like the final version?

Mary: Chapter 13 is AI Insights, and I was reading the Overview - it seems paragraphs 2 and 4 are too similar - What do you think?

ChatGPT: After reviewing the provided excerpts from the "AI Insights" chapter, it does appear that paragraphs 2 and 4 share similarities in their themes and content. Both paragraphs emphasize Mary and ChatGPT's exploratory journey into AI, its impact, and potential future implications.

Paragraph 2 focuses on the diverse applications of AI in various fields and its transformative role, highlighting the dialogues between Mary and ChatGPT to understand AI's integration into everyday life.

Paragraph 4, while it starts with a slightly different angle, stating the chapter as a "journey of discovery," eventually converges to a similar theme. It talks about exploring AI's impact and future implications, mirroring the notion of comprehensive exploration found in paragraph 2.

The redundancy seems to arise from both paragraphs covering the exploratory nature of Mary and ChatGPT's discussions about AI, its impact, and its future. To enhance the distinctiveness of each paragraph, you might consider focusing paragraph 2 more narrowly on specific examples of AI applications. In contrast, paragraph 4 could emphasize their discussions' speculative and forward-looking aspects, concentrating more on AI's future possibilities and ethical considerations. This would create a clearer differentiation between the current state of AI (as discussed in paragraph 2) and the future potential and challenges of AI (as highlighted in paragraph 4).

BOOK COVER COMMENTS – PRE-LAUNCH

I am not a graphic designer, but I love a challenge with new software. I used Canva, and with ChatGPT's instructions, I pulled together a book cover concept and sent a copy out to friends and family for comments and opinions.

The comments are listed in the order that I received them. It was great that the first comment was so positive!

- I love the coloring and sparkly glimmer of it. Yes, I think it would be a very attractive book cover.
- I love the look of that!
- Looks ok to me.
- Like the concept. It makes me want to read more. You're a talented author. (from my best friend)
- It is good. I would change the typeface on the front so that the white text has a black outline or shadow so that it is easier to read against the background.
- Love This! (Emoji)
- Very nice. I like.
- Really professional
- Very interesting
- Love (Emoji)
- Well, I am an absolute analphabet regarding AI but reading the introduction seems to give us a perspective on how we can use AI and live with this new reality.
- I like the design and colors. I feel like the title should have a colon or something separating the two parts. (from an English teacher).

AUTHOR'S MESSAGE

As I step back from my desk, I'm filled with gratitude. This book, born from my conversations with ChatGPT, has been a unique and surprising journey, made possible by your support and enthusiasm.

Your interest, comments, and encouragement have been crucial. They inspired me to delve deeper into the fascinating world of AI interactions, turning some of our exchanges into the pages you've just read.

Seeing how my words and ideas have resonated with you has been the greatest joy of my writing journey. Your positive response has been both humbling and inspiring.

Thank you for being a part of this adventure. It's your engagement that has brought these conversations to life and made this book what it is.

Sincerely,

Mary Louise Hill

JOIN ME ON SOCIAL MEDIA

Amazon Author Page
https://www.amazon.com/author/talkingwithmary

Talking with Mary YouTube Channel
https://www.youtube.com/@TalkingWithMaryEng
Don't forget to like and subscribe!

Facebook
https://www. facebook.com/talking.with.mary

LinkedIn
https://www.linkedin.com/in/mary-lou-hill-b5a758b1

OTHER TALKING WITH MARY BOOKS

Quick Grammar Refresher (Exercises Only)

Quick Grammar Refresher Book 2 (General Theme)

Quick Grammar Refresher Book 3 (Travel Theme)

Quick Grammar Refresher Book 4 (Dining Theme)

Idioms from Three Generations Book One

Coming soon
    Idioms from Three Generations Book Two